PRIDE IN ENGLAND

PRIDE
IN ENGLAND

A Rugby Autobiography

Roger Uttley

with David Norrie

STANLEY PAUL
London Melbourne Sydney Auckland Johannesburg

To my folks for giving me such a good start and to Kris
for getting me through some traumatic times … as you are
about to find out

Stanley Paul & Co. Ltd

An imprint of the Hutchinson Publishing Group

17–21 Conway Street, London W1P 5HL

Hutchinson Group (Australia) Pty Ltd
30–32 Cremorne Street, Richmond South, Victoria 3121
PO Box 151, Broadway, New South Wales 2007

Hutchinson Group (NZ) Ltd
32–34 View Road, PO Box 40-086, Glenfield, Auckland 10

Hutchinson Group (SA) Pty Ltd
PO Box 337, Bergvlei 2012, South Africa

© Roger Uttley and David Norrie 1981

First published 1981

Set in VIP Baskerville by
Computape (Pickering) Ltd, Pickering, North Yorkshire

Printed in Great Britain by The Anchor Press Ltd
and bound by Wm Brendon & Son Ltd,
both of Tiptree, Essex

ISBN 0 09 146320 3

Erratum

P. 116 3rd line to read:

Following that conversation, commonsense prevailed
on both sides. Bob sent through a cheque on behalf
of the RFU and, thankfully, once more all was well.

Contents

Acknowledgements

I should like to thank David Norrie for his invaluable help in writing this book and keeping me at it when the going got tough during those long winter nights.

Photographic Acknowledgements

Copyright photographs are acknowledged as follows: *Blackpool Gazette & Herald* Ltd; Mike Brett; Central Press Photos Ltd; Colorsport; Michael John Cornish; *Evening Standard*; Fleet Fotos; George Herringshaw; *Lancashire Evening Post*; John T. Learwood; *Manchester Daily Mail*; D. Gordon Swinton; Bob Thomas

I

Grand Slam Day

15 March 1980 ... the greatest day in English rugby for quarter of a century was upon us. At long last, the agonizing wait was over. The burning question now was: 'Were we good enough to beat Scotland and thereby clinch the Grand Slam?'

In the changing room at Murrayfield, there was no doubt in my mind. I was looking at the lads who were going to bring England their first championship since 1963, their first Triple Crown since 1960 and their first Grand Slam since Eric Evan's magnificent effort in 1957. Paul Dodge hadn't even been thought of then and I was still struggling through the basics of addition and subtraction. Those days were long gone; nobody then had heard of decimalization, defection, devolution, deodorants, de-centralization and deep throat.

But, even though none of us had been playing in 1957, we had all been, at various times, targets of abuse for England's disastrous seventies. My close companions in the dressing room were all fellow travellers of long standing and special friends. Was it really nine years since Wheelbrace (Peter Wheeler), Jaws (Fran Cotton), Nero (Tony Neary) and myself set off as raw recruits on England's 1971 Far East tour?

We'd just about reached the other end of our playing lives now. Even with over a hundred caps between us and several Lions tours, our long trek would mean nothing if we were beaten today. I think we would have been prepared to give away all we had achieved for this single victory.

For myself, I'd embarked on this 'now-or-never' crusade several months earlier. My career was in cold storage at the time, with no clues as to whether my neglect was likely to be permanent. Twice I'd been captain of England, and twice I'd

9

lost it! Injury and illness were the reasons, and in my latter days there was always a question mark over my fitness.

In my opinion, this particular warhorse was good for another season yet. I thought I had proved my point when I helped the North to defeat Graham Mourie's All Blacks at Otley, but I was left on the bench for the international against New Zealand the following Saturday. Luckily. the selectors swallowed their pride for the start of the Five Nations championship and slotted in the correct pieces of the jigsaw. John Horton also returned to the side at fly-half and the final answer to our problems came in the considerable presence of Phil Blakeway at prop. For once England had chosen a side that the players thought was the best available. Such a rare event was bound to create some memorable occurrence.

Our crushing defeat of the much-fancied Ireland was the perfect start. And the England supporters who travelled to Paris for our match with France must have been hoarse as we made it two out of two. Then we collected the hat-trick when Wales was beaten by a single point. Unfortunately, the result was not what remained in people's minds for they witnessed a sorry spectacle, with rugby taking a back seat to brawling and bad feeling. Paul Ringer was sent off by David Burnett after a quarter of an hour. His departure did little to cool tempers. I suppose his subsequent canonization by the Welsh was only to be expected. Within days, fans were wearing badges declaring: 'Paul Ringer and Hissing Sid are innocent!' Well, I've had my doubts about Captain Beakey and his Band, but Ringer was guilty as charged.

Just before half-time I also left the field, though not at the referee's insistence. Geoff Wheel mistook my head for the ball and my own participation in this orgy of violence was over.

Fortunately, there was a month to the Scotland clash: if Murrayfield had been only a fortnight away, then there would have been no chance of my playing. Nothing unusual, so far as Scotland's national ground was concerned; despite being an international player of eight years' standing, this was to be my first and last appearance there. Again, it was an injury, not selectors' whims, that had contrived to keep me from Murrayfield.

10

So you can understand my relief when I found myself on such hallowed turf during the pre-match walkabout. Only a handful of spectators speckled the terraces at this stage, but already the tension was beginning to build up. Nervous though the atmosphere was, our mood was confident, as it had been in the England camp all through the season.

The immediate build-up had begun the previous Wednesday night. Heathrow was the congregating point for the Southerners and West Country lads who were to fly up to Edinburgh on Thursday morning. During lunch at the North British we were joined by Bill Beaumont's boys from the north. Then we all took the coach to Peebles for a work-out under coach Mike Davis.

With my history of back trouble, I was always glad to get through a session without any reaction. That afternoon I felt so good that I set off for a run around the back of the Hydro with Maurice Colclough. As I plodded up the winding paths and down the valley, the tensions and pressures of international rugby seemed a million miles away.

Relaxing in a warm bath back at the hotel, I was almost worried because the team was feeling so good and so well prepared. My room-mate in Peebles was Tony Neary; I'd known him longer than anyone else in the side – basketball brought us together in about 1964. We talked of the future, but agreed there was one last job to do. We had to be totally committed to this one game, otherwise everything else would seem a total waste of time.

The following morning, after a gentle work-out, we travelled to Edinburgh. During lunch in the North British, Alan Old pointed out that nobody had planned anything for 'Old Snowy'. Old Snowy was Tony Neary and the game against Scotland was his forty-third cap, making him the most-capped English player of all time. My guilt feelings were shared by Bill Beaumont, so we quickly organized a whip-round. Alan and I found a trophy shop which engraved a tankard for us. Bill and I picked it up on the Saturday morning.

Friday night is film night on international weekends. In Edinburgh we watched an old favourite, *The Mean Machine*, in which Burt Reynolds leads a team of convicts to victory over

11

the prison guards in a game of American football – plenty of blood and guts, though liberally sprinkled with the ironic humour which is an essential part of any intense sporting confrontaton. We needed to win as badly as the cons. They had been written off by society. We'd been written off by many people as not good enough to win the Grand Slam. Well, tomorrow would prove them wrong.

As we all wandered off to bed, I could feel the team 'bubbling' – eager, not apprehensive, for tomorrow. It's the stairs for me the night before a game, not the lift. Bounding up two or three flights reassures me about my fitness. Last-minute withdrawals are never far from my thoughts. Normally, only the captain gets a single room, but for some reason I wasn't sharing that night. Sleeping before big games has never bothered me and I was soon well away. Waking is no problem, either, as I like to get up and check the body is functioning properly.

Breakfast is a major event. Forwards generally need a good feed – grapefruit, two eggs, a mixed grill, toast and marmalade, washed down with tea. Other early risers include Phil Blakeway, Ian Peck and Alan Old; the rest of the lads usually drift in as we are finishing. Some players, like Steve Smith, you never see; he's too busy lying in bed watching 'Tiswas' and 'Swapshop'. Steve Smith, did at least make the team meeting at eleven o'clock, when Mike Davis briefed us, helped by the now familiar overhead projector. Its initial appearance had caused a few raised eyebrows, what with his key words and all. We weren't back at school and he wasn't going to form much of a teacher-pupil relationship with the England rugby squad. But, since that hesitant start, we had learned a lot about one another. Mike became more forthcoming and began to consult us, while our trust and respect increased as his ability emerged.

But today there wasn't a lot left to say. All the talking had been done before the Welsh game. Now it was a question of getting on the park and doing the business. And doing it in a manner that would exorcize the memory of that Twickenham brawl from our minds. We must win ... by playing good rugby.

After lunch we bundled into the coach for the journey along Princes Street to Murrayfield. The roads were lined with the Tartan terrors; the rugby variety remain good-humoured, but they would have liked nothing better than to see us go under today. So far as we were concerned their threats of 'we'll hammer you' were based on nationalistic pride, certainly not on sound rugby judgement. That journey is an essential part of the atmosphere in Edinburgh, as are the besieging autograph hunters in the ground once we get off the bus. For the time being, other matters were pressing and the youngsters were rather brusquely ignored. No offence meant; see you afterwards – if we win!

Inside I grabbed a spot near the old-fashioned gas heaters. It was pleasing to find several greetings telegrams waiting for me. One was from my mother and father; they had spared no sacrifice over the years to help in my sporting aspirations. Another was from my new club, Wasps. Their kindness had been an important factor enabling me to settle comfortably in the south.

After the early pitch inspection, we wandered inside to get changed. We might not see much of Steve Smith at breakfast, but the bloke was always first on the couch of the physio, Don Gatherer. Even before I had taken my teeth out, he was stripped and ready to succumb to Don's magic fingers. Eventually, though, Don was rubbing the deep heat into my lumbar regions, then he piled on plenty of grease to keep my back warm.

Everybody was nearly ready and Bill took us out for the photograph. The crowd was increasing rapidly and becoming noisy. We trotted back to the changing room for the final time with about twenty-five minutes to go. Inside, Mike Davis was prowling around like a caged animal. His job was done; it was up to us now. No matter how much he would have liked to be running out there with us, he was committed to sweating it out with the other selectors in the stand.

The clock moved slowly towards three o'clock. Alan Old led the replacements to their places. We were left alone as the countdown began, just the fifteen with Mike. All the hopes and dreams of a rugby nation lay with us – and we knew it.

13

But, looking around at the rest of the lads, I knew we weren't going to blow it, not this time. This England side wasn't about to let go. Reaching to this point had been a real team effort. All fifteen and one or two others had played a full part in making today possible. From Dusty at full-back right through to Phil Blakeway at prop, everybody knew his job and did it well.

Not long to go now as we waited for French referee Monsieur Bonnet's tap on the door. French officials normally allow a flowing game, which was what we wanted, but we had to be careful that this did not lead to our downfall. Over-confidence might allow the Scots to run amok in Murray-field's wide open spaces. The Scots, with the effervescent Andy Irvine directing operations from full-back, had nothing to lose. What pleasure it would give them to deny the 'auld enemy' their long-awaited Grand Slam. They'd shown what they were capable of in the game against France. Recovering from a 4 points to 14 deficit, the Scots scored 18 points in the last thirteen minutes to end their run of thirteen internationals without a win. Andy, who had been in a terrible state in the first half, was the instigator of the revival with two tries and 16 points – a new record for a Scot. So we had to be on our guard.

Bill took us through our various stretching exercises before we huddled together for his final words of encouragement. 'Come on, now. No mistakes by us, but we've got to punish theirs. Smithie wants good ball, no rubbish. Look, we've got to pull them in on the fringes; if they start standing off, then we drive forward again to make sure they're committed. Right!'

Like a telephone suddenly ringing, the knock on the door snatched our attention. Referee Bonnet ran his hands over our studs to check they were not dangerous. Eyes met; a mutual look of determination. Just one more time; no mistakes. Come on, let's go; and seconds later we were running out to a tremendous roar, with Dusty bringing up the rear as usual.

Now the ground was full. The crowd made even more noise when the blue-shirted warriors took the field. The huddle of white jerseys got together for the national anthem. I defy the Welsh to sing with any more gusto than we did that day. There may be Englishmen who are not as patriotic as the Scots, Welsh or Irish, but none of them was on the

Murrayfield pitch as we prepared to give everything for our country.

Suddenly, all the singing and talking were over. It was time for action. My memories of the game are rather vague. The pace of play was exceptional, even for an international. Yet, rather than wait the whole eighty minutes, we managed to clinch the Grand Slam in the first half hour. By then we had put together three magnificent tries. Whatever the Scots tried now, there was no way we were going to let them get back into the game as the French had done.

The power of our pack made it possible for the backs to cut loose for once. Clive Woodward was the 'hammer of the Scots' – as he would be a year later in the same fixture. Showing a running ability that is rugby's greatest rarity, Clive twice scythed his way through a bemused Scottish defence to make tries for John Carleton and Mike Slemen. Our strong scrum created another try for John Carleton when John Scott picked up at number eight. Dusty added the conversion points for the first two scores and our opening surge had taken us 16 points ahead.

The Scots, never ones to take defeat lightly, set about running us off our feet in the second half. Before they got into their stride, there was very nearly a moment of glory for me just after the interval. Steve Smith had set John Scott off near the Scottish line and I was in support to take his return pass. Just for a moment the line seemed within my grasp, but I was brought down by a thundering tackle. Without thinking, I flung back a terrible pass to Steve Smith; it was absolutely dreadful and could have gone anywhere. Luckily, Steve only has to sniff a try. He took the pass above his head to dive over. I was relieved, he was delighted and England were safe at 23–3.

The Scots stepped up the pace even more. The score quickly became 23–12 before Andy Irvine, always just as likely to lose games as to win them, misjudged a kick by Paul Dodge. John Carleton couldn't have asked for a better bounce as he raced away for the first hat-trick of tries by an English international since 1924. An earlier Dusty penalty meant the score was now 30–12. The Scots had the final word with a superb solo try by fly-half John Rutherford. Irvine's conversion made it 30–18, but we had done it!

My initial reaction at the final whistle was relief – I had pulled a rib cartilage whilst attempting to tackle Keith Robertson midway through the second half. With Tony Neary also suffering from a badly bruised calf, the English back row had just about run out of steam. In my case the pain was bad and, after a brief encounter with Don Gatherer on the touch-line, I had been in two minds as to whether to go off. But Bill pressed me to stick it out. After all, I had left the field in England's previous two internationals – three in a row would have been an unenviable record. So I stayed on, although I'm not sure how effective I was in those dying minutes.

When the final whistle went, we all bolted for the changing rooms. In the tunnel the Scots looked disappointed; but they shouldn't have done. There was no disgrace in a defeat like this. Our faces were dominated by huge grins as we beamed 'Well done' and 'Congratulations' to one another.

Back in the dressing room the celebrations began. The 'alikadoos' were out in force, as is usually the case when we've won. Regulars, like Tarn Bainbridge and John Burgess, would always pay their respects over the years, win or lose. But on a day like this we were tolerant of everyone.

After a great victory, I always get a sense of anticlimax. The extent of our achievement was obvious to me, but I'd played in tougher games and this was just another match. Such depression builds up because you are drained physically and mentally, not only by the game itself, but by all the pre-match atmosphere and tension. You tend to look around the room and wonder, 'Why the hell is everybody getting so excited?'

But the champagne was now flowing and rightly so; we'd done England and English rugby proud. As usual, the veteran quartet had more serious things on its mind. Tony Neary was putting an ice-pack on his calf, Fran and Peter were holding a mutual appreciation society general meeting congratulating each other for having taken the opposition apart. As for me, I was lighting up a long-awaited cigarette!

2
Early Days

Back to the beginning. I was christened Roger Miles Uttley and made my debut appearance on 11 September, 1949. My first fighting weight, as befits a future England forward, was a more-than-healthy 10 pounds. Despite Northumberland rumours to the contrary, I'm a Lancashire lad, born and bred in Blackpool.

I was the middle one in our own particular battle of the sexes, sandwiched between two sisters; Jane, who was four years older than me, and Deborah, who arrived seven years after me. My folks, Stuart and Peggy, still live in the house in Devonshire Road where I spent a happy childhood. My father then worked for a local firm of gents' and ladies' outfitters, W. H. Orry; today he is a director.

My earliest Second World War and Wild West adventures took place on an old golf course which belonged to the Norbeck Hydro Hotel. Even when the bulldozers moved in, I was more than happy with the re-designed assault course, especially when the kind workmen took care constantly to add new sections for me to investigate. Naturally, there were plenty of bumps and bruises to be had and about this time I started scarring that famous quarry known as my face. No, I haven't always looked like this!

Soon I was to discover one of the most important facts of life ... school. The local education authority had earlier ruined the beautiful view of the fells from our house by building an establishment for the teaching of young boys and girls. As way of compensation, I was to become a regular attender there. At least I could look at the fells again.

Fortunately, the summer holidays seemed to last for ages.

The beach at Norbeck was only three-quarters of a mile away. Unless snow was falling, we'd try and organize a family outing down to the sands every Sunday; when school was out, then every day was Sunday.

The ritual of Sunday was never upstaged. Even the impatient wait to get underway was as much a part of the tradition as the sand in the sandwiches. Why do parents delight in taking such a cruelly and unnecessarily long time in getting ready to go out? Eventually, with enough food to feed the five thousand – egg-with-salad sandwiches were my favourites – we were ready for the off.

The journey had familiar landmarks at every turn. By the time we turned the corner at the chip shop, the sun (when available) was glinting off the sea. This was the spot where our heavily laden parents were left behind as the youngest generation of Uttleys made a sprint for the sand. Even in those early days, the side-step was in evidence as we dodged the traffic on Queen's Promenade.

The perfect execution of this skill belonged to my sister Jane. My initial reaction to anything in front was to duck my shoulder and charge on. Handy on a rugby field, but not the wisest course of action for a nine-year-old who wants to reach ten. But, once over the road, there were no further obstacles as we scampered over the tram tracks and detoured at speed to the very edge of the cliffs to answer the most important question of the day: was the tide in, or out?

Then, with shoes and socks coming off as we ran, there was at last that delicious feeling of sand under our feet.

Momentarily some concern for our folks returned, but only to make sure that the food was safe. Like the kings bearing gifts, they were searching for a protective buttress. Why don't parents like the windswept open spaces on beaches? They're always looking for shelter, mumbling something about sand getting in their faces and hair.

The beach was the scene of some of my earliest sporting encounters. The name we gave to our particular game was Rug-sock. Basically, what started out as football ended up a very robust form of rugby. My father worked on Saturdays, so these matches provided a rare opportunity to see him in action. Quite a stylist he was, too. Since those days, I have been very grateful that he taught me to swim. In the dark months when my back crippled me, it was about the only exercise I could manage.

The finer points of Rug-sock left us covered in sand. Before we were allowed near the moist sandwiches, a quick dip was compulsory. Then we stuffed ourselves to make the perfect end to a perfect Sunday.

Sometimes, outside the family environment, my large frame caused me problems in my teens. I was always head and shoulders above other kids of my age. Being rather shy and introverted, I tended to back away from the teasing, and drifted around with older boys. Until my sporting achievements helped give me a standing within the community, I suffered from the chronic 'big man' syndrome – always trying to melt into the background and adopt as low a profile as possible. Hopefully, though, the experiences haven't left any permanent scars.

Sport began to dominate my life at Montgomery Secondary School, but rugby took third place to cycling and basketball.

Cycling was my real devotion in my early teens. My commitment to the sport took me to the Fleetwood Road club with my friend Mike Gadd. Now we really found out what a gruelling sport it could be; the compensations, however, have been plentiful. The self-discipline, especially, has been a great service when I have needed to fight my way back to fitness for rugby. When you have to get up at five in the morning in cold, miserable rain for 'pleasure', you quickly develop a mental toughness and singlemindedness; these were needed in great doses during my problems in the seventies.

The object of all my love and affection at this time was Helyet. Well, a Helyet special, stainless steel spokes and all, Like most objects of affection, it proved expensive to keep. Mike and I worked in a local market garden – back-breaking work – to pay our way and keep the bikes in peak condition. The opening event of our first season as serious riders was the Circuit of the Dales. Mike and I had been training hard through the winter, but we were totally unprepared for the torture that lay ahead.

The dawn patrol was enough to put you off for a start. Time trials take place when there's no traffic about, so I was out of bed by 4.30 a.m. ready for a 6 a.m. start. Not that I suffered on my own. My poor dad was there to drive us in his Austin A40 with our bikes on the roof rack. The circuit is thirty miles, from Ingleton to Sedbergh to Hawes and then back to Ingleton.

During the first section, the relatively level route and the superb scenery combined to lull this novice into the false assumption that he had got this taped. But my legs had no interest at all in the picturesque views as I struggled up the hills at Garsdale between Sedbergh and Hawes.

Somehow, despite passing and being passed by other competitors, I was left with a horrible sense of isolation – me against the world. Two-thirds completed, one-third to go, but would my body last out? As I passed my dad on the side of the road, I told him I'd had it; but he told me to hang on and we would link up further on. Sure enough – and he never let me down – ten minutes later there he was at the side of the road with a jar of energy-producing honey. How he managed to conjure that up in the middle of nowhere, I'll never know. But, like Popeye with his spinach, the honey did the trick for me and I survived to reach the finish.

At Montgomery Secondary School, I came in contact with the next important influence on my life. Bryn Jones, the PE master, had been a scrum-half for Fylde but was now playing rugby league for Halifax. His expansive outlook on life and his love of open-air pursuits made a distinct impression on me, especially as he was more than willing to share his interests with his pupils. His commitment extended outside the normal school sporting curriculum to organizing school outings around the countryside. Since those days, finding relief and relaxation by walking over hills and fields had been my safety valve from the intensity of international sport.

Rugby was still lagging behind cycling and basketball in my list of priorities. My height especially was an asset in basketball and I was fortunate enough to make the North of England under-fifteen schools team.

In fact, my rugby aspirations suffered a fairly severe setback, all courtesy of my own foolishness. Again, my size was the main reason for reaching the final trial for the North's area school rugby side at under-fifteen level. But the weather was atrocious on the morning of my big day, with the wind howling and pools of water all over the garden. The venue was Hutton School, near Preston and only twenty miles away. My assumption that the trial would be postponed was badly miscalculated. While my immediate representative career was coming to an abrupt halt, I was at home congratulating myself on saving a wasted journey. Worse was to follow. Bryn Jones blew his top when he asked me how I had got on. In no uncertain manner, I was told that I had let down the school, my parents, and him – as well as myself. At least that lecture made its mark. Regardless of wind, rain, snow or earthquake, I could be guaranteed to turn up from that point on.

Bryn Jones's influence extended to my career plans: I decided to become a physical education teacher. That choice was a mixture of respect for him and respect for the life he led. Until then I had paid little attention to the academic side of school life, always looking to sport as my escape from work. Bryn pointed out that sport alone would not get me through college, nor would my current philosophy prepare me adequately for the rigours of the outside world. But this dressing-down carried with it the offer of help if I was serious in my intentions.

My academic work did show some signs of improvement, but tailed off when sport began to dominate again. In 1965, I was the proud recipient of the F. E. Harrison Trophy, awarded to the outstanding schoolboy sportsman in Blackpool. Credit for this must go to my basketball and cycling achievements, rather than any rugby prowess. But slowly the oval ball began to assert itself, as appearances for the Fylde Falcons, the club's schoolboy side, became a regular habit. What with school games, this often meant two matches on a Saturday. Because of all my other leisure pursuits, the fifth year at Montgomery was not the intensive period of study it should have been.

21

By the time O levels came round, I was in a state of panic, confronted by the inescapable fact that I hadn't done enough work. By then it was too late to do much about it. Waiting for the results was a speculative affair on a par with backing an outsider in the Grand National. Two passes out of four was about as much as I could have hoped for; that total could have ended my career ambitions there and then.

Fortunately, the grammar school at Blackpool opened its doors and offered me a lifeline chance to re-sit before I tried for a college place. What if they hadn't? Well, I've often wondered that, and the same worrying answer always emerges: I don't know!

Luckily several other lads from Montgomery also made the transfer, so I wasn't a total stranger in a new place. Those two years at Blackpool made me reasonably confident of emerging into the outside world. Rugby was the number one sport at the schools, as it became in my life. Jack Quarmby was the master in charge and came from a totally different mould than did Bryn Jones. Quieter and more restrained, his methods were equally effective. He tried to make me think more about the game; there must have been a flicker of hope because I was made captain of the first fifteen in my final year. My responsibilities didn't end there as I was also appointed head boy of the school. These positions did wonders for my self-confidence as I gradually felt able to assert myself individually. Whilst still big, I was no longer the giant I had been in my early days and didn't feel such an outcast.

To some, though, I remained too soft and unassuming on the rugby field. After a Lancashire schools trial, I was the subject of discussion between Bryn Jones and Dennis Chapman, an ex-prop from Preston Grasshoppers and involved on the county scene. They had got together after another 'powder-puff' display by young Uttley. 'Don't be so nice,' I was told, 'get stuck in more.' I tried to take their advice to heart, but physical aggression still worried me – especially when I was the victim! Getting into fights was not my scene, and I preferred to try to negotiate my way out of trouble.

The start of my more conscious approach coincided with the beginning of my schoolboy representative honours. I made the Lancashire schools side at number eight during my opening year in the sixth form at Blackpool. Also packing down in the back row was the captain, one Tony Neary, whom I had already come across in my basketball travels. Steve Kindon, who later found soccer fame with Burnley, was also in the team. Unfortunately, our Battle of the Roses against Yorkshire, who included future England fly-half Roger Shackleton in the centre, ended in a scoreless draw. Tony, who was in his final year, went on to captain England Schools.

My turn came the following year, in 1968. By this time, I was in the lock position and had been given the task of leading the Lancashire pack. Basketball and cycling were drifting into neglect. The switch to rugby may have seemed a natural progression, but at the time making that choice was not straightforward for me. Initially, cycling had seemed the area that I might achieve most success. As well as holding the title of British Cycling Federation Schoolboy Champion for the Lakeland District, my form had taken me to twentieth place out of 120 in a national time trial over twenty-five miles. Furthermore after captaining Blackpool Schools at basketball, I went forward for a final England trial. Asked by a local paper at the time about my sporting loyalties, my reply was rather presumptuous: 'I prefer basketball to rugby because it is constructive sport, whereas rugby is primarily a destructive one.' There have been several times over the years when I've had to agree with that judgement.

My selection for the England Schools rugby side was the deciding factor. Our eleven-day tour in April 1968, when we played three internationals, opened my eyes to the privileges of being in a rugby community and the possibilities that it offered. Touring around the world, meeting people in different places, was the biggest opportunity and I still rate travelling as rugby's greatest gift to its participants. Without rugby, there is no way I would have travelled the world once, let alone twice.

We built up quite a camaraderie over those games against Wales, Scotland and France. It has always amazed me how quickly you can build up real team spirit and how success or failure affects different individuals.

The highlight of this short schoolboy tour was a visit to Chartreuse in France, but we met Wales and Scotland first. Ted Parfitt was the man in charge and I was pleased to have an ally in Dennis Chapman on the management side.

As you can imagine, playing against Wales at schoolboy level was as full-blooded as a real international. That's not surprising when my opponent in the line-out was none other than Allan Martin. His friendly warnings about too much English competition for the ball were evident even then. Other well-known names in the Welsh side included Robert Dyer, Jim Shanklin and Keith Hughes.

We were beaten . . . a foretaste of what was to follow in later years. But we fought hard and the only difference between the two sides was a first-half penalty goal by Robin Williams. The match received plenty of national press coverage; I've kept John Reed's report from the Sunday Express, basically because it's complimentary. The relevant passage reads; 'Blackpool's Roger Uttley, who has appeared for Fylde, impressed me with his vigour and enthusiasm.' Since then I've always rated John as a shrewd judge of new talent!

The following Wednesday we saw off Scotland's challenge under floodlights at Kingsholm. The press really did get carried away the next day, saying England had at last found the next generation to do the job. They wouldn't have been so certain if they'd caught a glimpse of me next morning. I was going through my initial trauma of recovering from an excess of alcohol – i.e. a hangover – piled on top of hard physical exertion. I'd be foolish to try and convince you it was the last time it ever happened. But it was the first; and venturing into the unknown avenues of body abuse was not a pleasant activity.

By the time of my first-ever jet flight over to France, I felt like a seasoned tourist. Sightseeing in Chartreuse confirmed my fast-growing opinion that this was the life for me. I made the conscious decision that whatever happened in the future, rugby touring was going to be part of it.

Fly-half Steve Trigg took over as captain, while I was made pack leader. Our journey had taken its toll and we found

ourselves 11 points down at half-time. But we pulled ourselves
together and fought back to earn an 11 points to 11 draw.

My rugby career at Fylde was flourishing, too. A month
before my England tour, I attained Fylde first fifteen status.
On my trek up to the big time once I'd left the Falcons, the
protective wing of the Saracens had been my temporary home.
This group of lags, under the committed leadership of Kevin
Chappell, enjoyed the game to the full, on and off the field.
Regrettably, it was time to leave the crèche and strive for
higher honours. The big date for me was 23 March, 1968 with
my debut for Fylde First Fifteen against Middlesbrough, who
included one Phil Horrocks-Taylor at fly-half and a young
Alan Old in the centre.

Number eight was my spot and I made the pick-up and
charge that led to the try which gave us a half-time 3 points to
nil lead. Unfortunately, the second half was one-way traffic
and we were well beaten by 3 points to 13. Some of the blame
could have been laid at the door of the Fylde goal-kicker, who
missed the conversion and several penalty attempts. Sadly,
I'm only being self-critical. It may surprise many people
today, but in my youth I was quite an accomplished and
prolific points-scorer with the boot.

You don't have to believe me, let the local paper's report of
our game with Halifax give proof. 'Uttley, in great kicking
form, landed the conversion from the touch-line.' With four
penalties, I kicked a total of 14 points in our 26 points to 11
victory.

But the ball didn't always fly so true; here are some adverse
comments. About a game against Preston Grasshoppers; the
paper said; 'Uttley had his chance to square matters with two
penalty shots, but could not find the right blend of power and
direction in his kicking on these occasions.' Aren't journalists
kind ... he could have been far more direct than that.

We travelled to Scotland to meet Heriot's. This time a
report read; 'Uttley missed a sizeable number of penalties,
much easier than his conversion of the try.' How about this
from the game against New Brighton: 'Alas, young Uttley,
Fylde's kicker, had not Hart's range or accuracy.' Shades of
the Yorick speech from *Hamlet* here.

25

The crunch, as far as my kicking was concerned, came at the beginning of the 1968–69 season when we were hosts to Coventry. The Midlands club had a host of famous names – David Duckham, Bill Gittings, Rodney Webb, Roger Creed, Tim Dalton and Jim Broderick – but after a summer of intensive practice I felt even they were ready to feel the full weight of the Uttley toe.

Well, that was the basic idea. The stage was set perfectly for an impressive performance with an audience that included two England selectors. But this particular goal-scoring machine watched in horror and disgust as every single kick veered away from its intended target. That was the end as far as I was concerned, and I decided to get on with my job among the forwards and leave the kicking duties to other glory-seekers. That's not to say that I don't still fantasize about slotting over a last-minute match-winning touch-line penalty to give England the Grand Slam.

All this rugby was proving rather time-consuming. My experiences with England Schools had pushed academic worries aside. But they could be neglected no longer, as I had to find a college that would accept me the following autumn. Wherever that was going to be, and I had no idea at this stage, rugby was the first priority.

The game had helped me to establish myself as an individual, and the joys of touring had opened up a brave new world. Also, rather naively I equated success on the rugby field with success in one's private and professional life. Everyone at Fylde seemed to enjoy a pleasing lifestyle and appeared fairly affluent. Instead of rugby offering a way into promising career, my somersault mind thought it might provide a route out of the daily grind.

I soon found out otherwise when my rugby ability did not bring automatic entry into the Cardiff College of Education. Although my interview was not all that it might have been, the practical went well and I came away happy. Their subsequent refusal was a bitter blow to my pride and my hopes. And, because they'd been my first choice, my other options soon went the same way. With the chance of not making any college at all looming large, I had only myself to blame. I remembered my 'O' levels; why hadn't I worked harder when I had the chance?

Fortunately, help was at hand in the form of David Brooks, my headmaster at Blackpool. He was concerned that his head boy might be college-less. So, with his north-east connection, he fixed up an interview for me at the Northumberland College at Ponteland, just north of Newcastle.

What an inspired choice that proved. The best things that happen to you are not mapped out, but left to chance. Moving to the north-east paved the way for my adoption as a Geordie, brought me a wife, family and home and linked my name with that of Gosforth.

The Cardiff interview experience left me better prepared for my interrogation by Ponteland lecturer Alex Robinson. Ponteland, not being a specialist college, did not receive too many applications from England schoolboy internationals. We seemed totally compatible, though, and I was overjoyed to be offered a place. After several worrying weeks, I had a future again.

With a place assured, my study reverted to its former slackness, and I left Blackpool with five O levels, but no As. Looking back, those results reflect my fickle attitude to scholastic demands; my mother, especially, was disappointed at her son's lack of concentration. Wasting these opportunities is something I've regretted since; but what was the point of trying to be somebody I wasn't cut out to be?

That summer between school and college was spent working the deckchairs on Blackpool front. A very prestigous job it was, too; you had to apply very early to stand a chance of getting in. The open-air freedom was marvellous, although it was chaos when it rained. Should you bring the chairs in, or leave them in the hope that the sun might return?

You had to be ever watchful of the inspectors who were patrolling to see that you didn't re-issue tickets to make some loose change on the side. Balancing up at the end of the day was a major financial exercise and something of a lottery. Finally for us weary workers it was the back room at the Clifton Hotel; a few pints and then a sobering cycle home.

Practising my beer drinking came in useful because it was

to be an essential part of the college syllabus, with the Union Bar the headquarters for most activities. Leaving home seemed to upset my folks more than me; the wrench was more than compensated for by my new-found freedom, especially as there was plenty of time for rugby.

Around this time I made my debut for the senior county side, but that was not half as pleasant as the introduction to college life. My selection came in the form of 'good news and bad news'. The good news was that I, at eighteen, was Fylde's youngest-ever Lancashire cap. The bad news was that our opponents were Ulster, in Ulster, with eight internationals and six of them British Lions. My opponent in the line-out . . . Willie John McBride! Their pack also included Syd Millar, Ken Kennedy and Ken Goodall, with Roger Young and Mike Gibson among the backs for good measure.

Fran Cotton was another who made his debut that day, but we couldn't help Lancashire to victory. We, and me especially, were taken to the cleaners and lucky to lose by only 25 to 6. There was no trouble from Willie John; I guess he didn't think I was worth the effort. As I stood alongside the great man in the line-out, we must have looked like a 'before and after' advertisement for a body-building kit. Still, it was certainly a memorable event for one so young. I little thought then that I'd get to know Willie John so much better in South Africa six years later.

I didn't play very well and that game was the beginning and end of my senior career with Lancashire. But the reasons behind this had nothing to do with form. Time off from college for that Ulster visit had been given rather grudgingly by my head of department, Phyllis Morgan. She granted permission with the proviso that this sort of thing would be the exception, not the rule.

Imagine my trepidation when I was selected for the final Lancashire trial the following week and I had to approach her again. Her refusal was no great surprise and it presented me with the perfect excuse for not turning out.

The more experienced Richard Trickey and Mike Leadbetter were paired in the senior side in the trial. With this partnership, I was going to struggle to make the side. Coupled with this, the move to the north-east presented me with a more convenient alternative. So I informed the selectors that I wasn't available for future consideration.

Strangely, it only took a week of college life for me to link up with Gosforth. I had played for the village team against the Gosforth Nomads, and the after-match refreshments brought a tentative inquiry about whether I would be interested in trying my luck with them. Well, as I had brought a letter of introduction from Fylde to Gosforth, everything fell into place. So began a whole new phase of my life as I came into contact with a club and group of lads who are amongst the best in the world.

Progress was swift because I made my first-team debut a fortnight later, partnering Jack Rowell in the second row against Huddersfield. Missing from the Gosforth pack that day was the Northumberland captain Tommy Hall, who had made a record-breaking forty-seventh appearance for the county the week before. He would normally have come back either at lock or flanker, but with me in the second row and David Parker, another exile from Fylde, in the back row, there was no place for Tommy; he must have thought these Fylde refugees had it in for him.

The north-east had a dearth of big forwards; this was the more convenient option I had up my sleeve when I turned away from Lancashire. Maybe, once again, I was taking the easy way out.

There was no doubt, though, that being a college student was the life for me. My course took me off the campus for long periods – walking in the Cheviots, canoeing on the Tyne and rock climbing on the Crag Lough at Hadrian's Wall.

Being without a car, getting to Gosforth for training could be a problem. Fortunately, one of the centres at the club, John Gray, lived in Ponteland and was usually able to help out. Occasionally, I was left to my own devices. Once I scrounged a lift from a second-year student called Paddy. His girlfriend – one of a group of sophisticated third-year inmates – wasn't too pleased at having her evening disrupted because of the inadequate travel arrangements of a first-year rugby lout.

This lout thought he had better try and be friendly, and

29

attempted to indulge in some pleasant conversation while Paddy was away getting the car. For once the Uttley charm was on target as I reflected upon the subject of the beautiful sunset there had been that evening. The topic struck a chord with this particular art student and was to have far-reaching consequences.

As you might have guessed, this was my first encounter with the girl who was to become my wife. Kristine later expressed amazement that this big rugby lump could appreciate and converse about anything other than sport. To me at the time, though, the lift was more important, as I strove to establish myself in the Gosforth first fifteen. The transition to senior rugby was not without its problems. That Christmas, the role of the young pretender in the line-out cost me two teeth, courtesy of Maurice Parker. We laugh about the confrontation now, and ever since I've worn a gum-shield. But the incident raised doubts in my mind about my ability to cope with the physical attitude and rigours of first-class rugby.

Another setback at the time was our match against Northern in the semi-final of the Northumberland Cup. Stan Stoker's dropped goal decided this battle of two great rivals in our favour, but rugby was the loser that day. This was my first taste of being involved in eighty minutes of rugby where the result alone mattered. I didn't like it at all, although I could appreciate the motive behind this intensity. Success is a necessary aspect of life, but so is keeping a sense of proportion.

Kris entered my life on a more serious level before the end of that first year. That was lucky for me, because she had finished her course and left to teach at Gillingham High School. My family had a chance to meet her when Kris and I attended my sister Jane's wedding, in July. The occasion also gave Kris a chance to see what she might be letting herself in for.

I was back on Blackpool front that summer with the deckchairs. More importantly, those months saw the acquisition of my first car, a great step for any young lad. The black Austin Cambridge was not the sleek, racey sports model I thought my cavalier image deserved, but it soon became my pride and joy. A careful lady driver, the one previous owner, had kept the car in beautiful condition; she might have wept at the sight of half a dozen various rugby shapes, with kit, all piling into her little car.

Returning to college that autumn, I knew my season of grace as a newcomer was over. Now I was expected to hold my own and bid for further honours. Pre-term appearances for Fylde found Lancashire inquiring about my availability, but Northumberland became my adopted county in the 1969–70 championship.

My gentle steps into the big time became a giant leap when I was selected for the North East Counties side to meet the touring South Africans. My joy was matched by a great deal of apprehension. Me playing against the mighty Springboks and names like Dawie de Villiers and Piet Greyling ... the Fylde Falcons seemed a long way away.

Matching my career path was winger Ted Littlechild. At schools level, we'd played together for Lancashire and England. Now, Ted was studying at Durham University, and he was eligible for the North East selection.

Our captain was Phil Carter, the rugged Yorkshire centre.

My nerves were obvious as we gathered to stay at the Gosforth Park Hotel on the Friday night. While determined to try and do myself justice and not let the side down, the importance of the occasion made me feel not entirely in control of my own destiny.

As well as worrying about the Springboks, we had the anti-apartheid demonstrators to contend with. They had been trying to disrupt the whole tour and our game was no exception. But the 500 or so remained relatively peaceful, although there seemed to be hundreds of policemen as we walked the mile to the ground.

The full horror of my impending ordeal became alarmingly apparent while I sat in the changing room looking at the match programme. My only relief was that the great Frik du Preez was being rested. I was not alone in my nervousness; several others were also playing in their biggest game to date, and the atmosphere was tense, to say the least.

Roger Arneil, the pack leader, assembled the forwards

31

together and directed our attentions towards the enemy. 'Cometh the hour, cometh the man,' was his battle cry. It must have worked – I charged onto the field in much the same manner as soldiers left the trenches to go over the top.

The confrontation was as tough as I had expected, but we fought doggedly for an 8 points to 5 lead at half-time. But the benefits of touring together became obvious after the interval, as the visitors gained control. Still, we kept in touch until the final twelve minutes, during which they scored 11 points to emerge winners by 24 points to 11.

We had acquitted ourselves well and, despite being absolutely drained, I was just happy to be alive and in one piece. The result, and my performance, did wonders for my self-confidence. Others were also pleased with my form; now I was beginning to believe that I might survive at the top level.

The North were starting their domination of English rugby that was to last throughout the seventies. Lancashire had been the early dominating force through the coaching of John Burgess. Northumberland made up lost ground with the involvement of coach John Elders, and Danie Serfontein. Early signs of a revival were shown in the 1970–71 county championship. With both Lancashire and Yorkshire to play away from home, few fancied Northumberland's chances.

Our crunch game came when we travelled to meet Lancashire at Fylde of all places. We had our backs to the walls for most of the match, but Brian Keenleyside clinched victory for us with an enormous penalty from inside his own half. Brian was our big kicking gun at the time, with Malcolm Young waiting to take over once he had retired.

Even today, the sight of that ball soaring high between the posts towards the clubhouse is still one of my fondest rugby memories. As a traitor returning to old haunts, the 15 points to 12 success was particularly satisfying. That pleasure only intensified in the clubhouse afterwards. The red rose is held in great regard at Fylde, and Northumberland aren't even worth the contempt Lancastrians feel for Yorkshire.

Now, living away from this boiling-pot of county fanaticism, it was interesting to observe this hotbed of commitment from the outside. A group of Lancastrians together can be an arrogant bunch, treating other rugby types as very inferior. But there was no denying that Northumberland were in the ascendancy that day and Lancashire were forced to swallow their immense pride.

We followed that up with victory over Yorkshire, which gave us the Northern title for the first time since 1936. Disappointingly, Gosforth was the venue for our semi-final defeat at the hands of Gloucestershire, but the cup run had put us back on the map.

The county's prominence meant that I was beginning to get noticed, too. Earlier in the season, I had played against the flamboyant Fijians up in the desolation of Lidgett Green in Bradford. We won that day, but my memories of those marvellous tourists come from their humiliation of the Barbarians at the Gosforth greyhound stadium. Seldom have I seen such mobile forwards; their handling and support play was the key to their annihilation of top-class opponents. The sight of talented British players being shown the ropes by these foreign so-called pupils was an enlightening experience.

More foreign opposition, this time in strength, arrived later that season as part of the 1971 RFU's centenary celebrations. This time Frik du Preez did not cancel our date, but he was only one of several worries as the President's Fifteen lined up against the North at Birkenhead Park. Partnering him was Ellie Cester in the second row, while the pack also included Greg Davis, Brian Lochore and Ian Kirkpatrick in the back row, with Hannes Marais adding considerable weight at prop. The backs weren't a bad bunch either, combining the skill of Dawie de Villiers, the power of Bryan Williams and the artistry of Jo Maso and Pierre Villepreux.

Not unexpectedly, we lost, but it was a marvellous match, which showed off the visitors' world-class skill to the full.

The season was drawing to a close; my thoughts, if not my devotion, returned to academic pursuits. This was my third and final year. As well as exam worries, those twin fears reappeared after three years to haunt me: 'Had I done enough? Where was I going from here?'

My preparations for the exams received a bitter pyschological blow when news reached me of the tragic death of Bryn

Jones. Now teaching at the Charlotte Mason College of Education in Ambleside, he had taken a group of girls to the Cairngorms. He died after he had rescued a girl who had fallen, and then got into difficulties himself. Bryn had been such an important influence that I felt a great sense of loss. The news was all the more devastating because he left his wife Celia with young twin boys. In many ways, I tried to shut the episode from my mind and have seldom referred to it.

I had to make a life for myself. After six enjoyable weeks of teaching practice at Whitehaven Grammar School, I found out that Whitley Bay Grammar School was looking for a teacher with an interest in rugby. The position was only for a year, but it fitted in well with another arrangement I was currently making – marriage.

Kris and I had become engaged the previous summer, but had decided to wait until we were both earning before getting married. Times were hard and money was tight. Luckily, my grandmother had left me her engagement ring and this convenient legacy solved a tricky problem.

We were married at St Gabriel's Church in Heaton, Newcastle, on 27 July, 1971, but not before Mick Mahoney, my best man and the Gosforth wing, combined with others to entice me down to the club for a traditional stag night. The only act of mercy shown was that they allowed this event to take place the penultimate night before my 'sacrifice'.

Our big day passed without too many hitches, although the honeymoon was something of a disaster. Our romantic country cottage on Holy Island was unavailable – so we rather naively allowed ourselves to be enticed towards the landlady's attractive alternative, a room in her 'quaint and picturesque' guest house.

To be honest we didn't arrive there in the best of humour. Someone had raided the car before we left and placed a kipper on the exhaust manifold. The heat from the engine on our journey up the A1 did the rest. By the time we discovered the source of the dreadful smell, it was too late. Unfortunately, the joke was lost on us – unlike the lingering smell of the kippers. So we were hardly in the best frame of mind on our arrival.

Our private fantasy accommodation turned into a private nightmare as we discovered the reality of the sales talk. 'Picturesque' meant old and primitive; 'quaint' meant too small to swing a cat. Not that the feline creatures were the problem: to cap it all, our wedding night was serenaded by the snoring outside our door of a large dog who appeared to have squatters' rights.

Still, our marriage could only get better, but I felt sorry for Kris that the occasion was not all it should have been. As for me, I had been offered the first of several all-expenses-paid trips abroad, courtesy of the Rugby Football Union. The news of my inclusion in England's touring party to visit the Far East had come during my teaching practice at Whitehaven and was a great surprise.

My cause had been helped by the 1971 British Lions tour, which meant that the English Lions – Bob Hiller, Peter Dixon, John Spencer, Stack Stevens, John Pullin and David Duckham – were not considered. Still, I was delighted to be blooded along with other young faces such as Tony Neary, Fran Cotton and Peter Wheeler. Looking after this mixture of youth and experience was Bob Weighill (manager), John Burgess (coach) and Budge Rogers (captain). Even today, all three continue to play important roles within the RFU. Burgess's appointment was seen as his chance to press his claims for the post the following season, and Lancashire's coach was very much under the microscope during this three-week expedition.

Kindly, the Northumberland education authorities gave me leave of absence, without pay. They weren't being mean; I had only been in their employment for a fortnight before I sloped away on the tour. Once away, it was difficult to contain my excitement; here I was on the plane as part of an England party with famous names like Nigel Starmer-Smith and Peter Larter. This is it, Roger Uttley, you've made it at last.

The rugby was hard, with the conditions almost as difficult to overcome as the opposition. Japan led three times in our first match at Osaka, and we only saved the day with a couple of late tries. Four days later in Tokyo, we struggled to beat them again; this time victory came by virtue of two penalties to one. Injuries were becoming a major problem. Chris Wardlow damaged his knee ligaments in that game and Peter Rossborough was concussed. Already, injury had ruled out Jim Broderick and David Roughley. The final match was against Ceylon, and by now we were down to only 19 fit players. In that game Alan Cowman played full-back, with Jan Webster the replacement covering all the back positions.

My playing memories of the trip are vague, but not so several off-the-field incidents. Arriving at Colombo airport, our confidence was hardly sky high when we saw the ramshackled Bedford bus that was supposed to take us to our hotel. Rather tentatively, we got in and our incredible journey began with the gear following behind in a truck. The next thirty minutes seemed like thirty hours. Despite the road being cluttered with pedestrians (some moving), cattle, cyclists, carts and other historical vehicles, our little Ceylonese driver's foot was rarely off the accelerator. We pondered on whether we wanted to see our fate or to close our eyes and wait for the inevitable crash.

Miraculously, nobody was injured in all this dodgem-driving and we arrived at the hotel safely. Mind you, the dining room was a sea of pale faces as we assembled for lunch. Our brief respite was interrupted by John Burgess demanding to know; 'Have we dispensed with training then?'

It was a rhetorical question. A hurried summit meeting took place between, Bob, John and Budge. The end result was no surprise to us. 'Get ready for a run-about.' Being a newcomer and just happy to be there, I obeyed without question. But several of the more experienced lads were resentful and felt he was being unreasonable. There was no mutiny, but the incident clouded our judgement of the man who was odds-on favourite to be the next England coach.

To a young player, John Burgess could be rather intimidating. His team-talk before my Lancashire debut against Ulster sticks in my mind to this day. John would back up his players to the hilt, protecting them in any way he could; his devotion was wholehearted. Many England supporters must wonder why, after such success with Lancashire, his time as coach of England was disastrous. John's problem lay in his dictatorial method of coaching. County players in the north would follow him blindly, basically because their experience was limited and they didn't know any better. Everyone knew and expected John, dressed in his traditional sheepskin coat and yellow scarf, his head covered by that Russian hat, to be cajoling and remonstrating from the touch line. These outbursts were part of the northern scene. But John didn't modify his style with the national squad, nor were his methods flexible enough when it came to dealing with players with a much wider rugby background.

Because of this, John was often at odds when dealing with England players. His squad sessions were hard and unrelenting even with England. When he was in charge, our weekends were reduced to nothing more than travelling and running. Foolishly, no respite was allowed us on the days leading up to an international. By being worked too hard on Thursdays and Fridays, the England team lost its edge before taking the field for the international. John Burgess stood or fell by his results. With Lancashire his record is exceptional; with England, his period in charge bordered on the verge of being a national disaster.

All this was way in the future. Back home it was John Elders, and not John Burgess, who was given the England job. The reason for this turn-about was said to be John Burgess's rigid style and methods, which ultimately led to the neglect of back play. But his rejection was still a surprise and it is as well to examine the statement made by Sandy Sanders, the chairman of England's selectors at the time.

We reached a decision on the type of game we wanted to play which would fully utilize the natural talent of the players available and produce for England the type of football which we are capable of playing at our best. With that in mind, we consider the most effective manner in which we can hope to achieve our objective is to ask John Elders, an England selector, to use the limited time available to hand to prepare the side. I wish to acknowledge the very real contribution given by John Burgess to the difficult [Far East] assignment – England did well to combat the temperature, humidity and travel problems with which they were confronted. There is no doubt that John Burgess did as much as any man could to .

prepare the side physically for the task.

Obviously, they didn't want John Burgess or his methods. With England's selectors desiring a more expansive game, then John Elders was the man they looked towards.

My Northumberland connection meant I knew John Elders almost as well as John Burgess and felt that my personal ambitions had not been harmed by his appointment. He was less demonstrative than Burgess and more introverted. Nevertheless, John Elders was responsible for several of us with the county team making the most of our talents with some small success.

When I had flown back from the Far East, having played in six of the seven matches – all won – I felt just about ready for my full cap. Arriving home in my tour blazer and carrying an airline bag covered in stickers, nobody was going to tell me that Roger Uttley was not an established part of the England rugby scene now. To my despair, though, my full cap was still eighteen months away. Many times through the next year and a half, I wondered if I would ever make it. At least, there was my new image to hang onto. During a county game against Cheshire at Sale, several of the lads were complaining about the heat. My 'It's not half as bad as Singapore' taunt was greeted with groans all round. Teams didn't travel the globe as much as they do today.

A treasured memory is my selection for the fifteen raised by Mickey Steele-Bodger to play Cambridge University in the autumn of 1971. With me in the second row was the now England coach Mike Davis; the side also contained several British Lions from that summer, including Mike Gibson. That Lions tour had done wonders for British rugby: at last the 'invincible' All Blacks were not unbeatable after all. Everybody back home was longing for a chance to see the Lions in action.

The players obliged that afternoon at Grange Road with a complete abandonment of the safety-first tactics I was used to with England. Initially I thought, if international rugby is like this, then I'm never going to be good enough. The pace of the game was frightening.

Back home, Northumberland's challenge was failing to maintain the impetus of the previous season. Shortly after, the North were beaten by the South and South West down at Exeter.

Coming back on the train, I managed to corner John Elders and proceeded to give him a right ear-bashing. How long will it be before I am capped? Will I ever make it? I told John that time seemed to be passing me by and that my career was not progressing as I thought it should. Such questioning obviously put him in an embarrassing position, but he had heard the anxious voice of youth before, and hinted that he didn't think I was quite ready yet.

The final trial offered little consolation. The Probable locks Nick Martin and Chris Ralston faced David Watt and Alan Brinn on the Possibles side. How highly rated was I? Well, I wasn't lost to the action and ran the line as touch-judge . . . so near and yet so far!

That 1972 championship season passed without even a non-travelling reserve card; up in Newcastle, I felt totally in exile. Luckily, the emergence of Gosforth as a major force in club rugby was more than adequate compensation. Big Jack Rowell, my minder in my early days, was now captain, and a whole stream of rugby orphans began turning up. David Robinson joined from Birkenhead Park after the England Far East tour. Soon other additions – including Peter Dixon, Colin White, Steve Gustard, and Terry Roberts – came from all directions. Hooker Duncan Madsen, like me, made the journey back from Fylde; and home-bred Brian Patrick made an immediate impact and joined his brother Harry in the first fifteen.

This pleasant group of players was together for nearly a decade. A family atmosphere developed at the club as this bunch of lads grew old together, maturing slowly like a fine wine. I believe this is the only way you can get a team to perform well over a period of time. England in 1980 created the same feeling, which is almost as though you have your own private side.

England in 1972, though, were at the other end of the success scale, and earned their first-ever whitewash in the championship. The forthcoming tour to South Africa that summer did not fill their supporters with too much optimism after such a humiliation. The selectors didn't seem too keen, either, because they had trouble finalizing the party of twenty-five. They released twenty-one names, saying that a final quartet would be added later. My name had been bandied about, but after my neglect I did not hold out much hope.

Yet my name was there in their postscript, and I was all set for a second successive summer abroad with England. The glaring omission was Chris Ralston, the lock forward who had played throughout the championship and had been hailed as one of England's finest discoveries for years. For some strange reason, he was out and my second-row companions were Peter Larter and David Watt.

That selection made up for all the disappointments of the season. So pleased was I that I put in some extra training sessions, taking advantage of some new weights the club had acquired. This conscientious behaviour proved my undoing. Something went in my leg as I did some squats; but the incident didn't seem serious and I thought nothing about it during a long soak in the bath.

Instead of resting the leg and taking medical advice, I foolishly tried to run the pain off. Luck wasn't on my side and the leg received a knock on the same spot when I played the following Saturday; now I was in real trouble. Time was running out and it was with diminishing confidence that I linked up with the rest of the party in London.

Leo Walkden, the RFU's doctor, who has seen me ridiculously often over the years, was in attendance. (If he had been treating me as a private patient, Leo would have retired to the South of France by now or be on his yacht somewhere in the Adriatic.) Examining my leg, he knew the injury was bad, but was kind enough to leave the decision to me as far as possible. He suggested a short sprint, knowing that this simple task would signal the end of my tour. He is seldom wrong. Within a few yards, I came to a shuddering halt as recognition of the awful truth could be delayed no longer. What a bitter moment ... only marginally helped by Leo's warning that another knock on the leg could be really serious.

Having to tell the manager, Alec Lewis, and John Elders and the rest of the lads was acutely embarrassing ... not only for me. They knew it could just as easily have been them. I felt that maybe I had come to London under false pretences and had not given them adequate time to find a replacement.

As they left Heathrow for South Africa, I flew back to Newcastle for another embarrassing moment; this time in the school staff room. After a grand send-off, here I was back again three days later. What a star rugby player they had!

But at least my bad luck signalled the return of Chris Ralston to the England fold; Lurch was to play a crucial part in the historic test win in Johannesburg.

England were the last of the home countries to tour South Africa. None of the others had been successful and an England side which was firmly embedded at the foot of the championship was expected to have little chance against the Springboks, who had won seven games on the trot. England leader for the tour was John Pullin. Peter Dixon, who had taken over the captaincy from Bob Hiller earlier in the year, was unavailable. Yet, despite a gruelling provincial schedule which they went through unbeaten and being the first home country to play a test at altitude, England celebrated an historic 18 points to 9 international victory at Johannesburg. With David Watt injured, there was every chance that I would have come in for my first cap that day to partner Peter Larter. There is also no chance that I would have contributed as much as Chris Ralston did that day; his line-out jumping was crucial. England, against all the odds, had picked themselves off the floor to revive dreams of a new era.

But would I be part of it? I tried to be philosophical about missing the tour and a possible cap; the delay gave me time to add the finishing touches to my game. Yet deep down inside, I worried that every time I seemed to have that England place within my grasp, something would happen to move it further away. Surely that couldn't go on for ever?

3

My First Cap ... Then We Beat the All Blacks!

England needed all the hopes of a new revival because Ian Kirkpatrick's All Blacks made a major tour of the United Kingdom in the winter of 1972–73. In those days the New Zealanders carried an invincible aura with them as they travelled England.

True, the British Lions had shown the way in the summer of 1971, but only the national team had ever beaten the All Blacks in England. Many thought they couldn't be beaten. As with the four-minute mile, a mental barrier existed and, until it was broken, all English sides were trying the impossible.

But beaten they were, on 22 November 1972, and the heroes at Warrington were the men of the North West led by Fran Cotton. If I had stayed in Lancashire, I might have been part of that triumph, but my challenges came from the east of the Pennines now. The North West's 16 to 14 victory left the North East with plenty to prove in their match with the tourists.

That was going to be a crucial match for me. Instead of starting the season as an England international, my position was one of 'maybe' with a lot of ground to make up. I was well aware that some players were only given one chance. Had I missed the boat? Chris Ralston's form in South Africa had made a mockery of his original omission. Lurch was the top line-out jumper in the northern hemisphere and had now proved his ability to compete with the best. No, if I was going to force my way in, it would be at the expense of Peter Larter. Obviously, he wasn't going to make that easy for me.

I took over the captaincy of Northumberland and enjoyed the experience of working closely with John Elders and Danie

42

Serfontein, coach and chairman of the selectors respectively. Unfortunately, the big two games – against Lancashire and Yorkshire – were lost, but the exercise was beneficial for me.

As preperation for the All Blacks' visit, a couple of training exercises were organized at Roundhay. Danie Sefontein arranged for a small coach to take the Northumberland lads down to Leeds. The bus was incapable of going any faster than twenty-five miles an hour, and, in addition, the coach driver, like all rugby coach-drivers, had no idea where his ultimate destination was. I've yet to meet one who knows where any rugby ground is, apart from Twickenham. So, as we cruised through Leeds, kerb-crawling, looking for a knowledgeable citizen, we came across a very small young man complete with sports holdall and umbrella. A likely victim; we stopped the bus and asked directions.

'Give me a lift and I'll show you the way.'

'Going there, too?'

'Yes.'

'What's your name?'

'Peter Squires!'

We were to have many great times together over the next few years. Although he later missed that All Blacks game because of injury, he became one of the North's star performers in the seventies. And he was the model of consistency in his twenty-nine consecutive appearances for England. If he has one regret, it was his decision to concentrate on his cricket career for Yorkshire and not tour with the 1974 Lions in South Africa. As it was, Peter toured with the 1977 party to New Zealand, but it was the conditions of South Africa which would have suited him best.

The Yorkshire selectors moved him around at the beginning of the 1979–80 season and these positional switches allowed John Carleton to win the battle for the right-wing spot for the North against the All Blacks. That marked the end of Peter's reign in the England team, which was a great shame because, with his laconic wit and simple outlook on life, he was far and away one of the most popular members of the national squad in the seventies.

But he was missing when we lined up against the New

43

Zealanders at Bradford, a week later after they had beaten Wales 19 to 16 in their first international. The 'Murdoch incident' had followed that match and the huge prop was soon on his way home, although it apparently took him a few more years to reach New Zealand. The tourists' morale was given another knock when David Duckham's Midland Counties West team beat them at Moseley. The North East fifteen were under the direction of Yorkshire's John Robbins, who had been coach of the ill-fated 1966 British Lions tour of South Africa led by Mike Campbell-Lamerton. I found him, yet another John, a very caring person and intelligent coach.

The All Blacks were almost at test strength that day, but we could have won. Instead the breaks went their way and we went down by 3 points to 9; the only break we received was when Grant Batty stepped all over David Carr's arm early on. The All Blacks, after all the problems of the past seven days, were happy to leave the field with a win.

But nothing could submerge the mood of ascendancy in the north, which we hoped would ultimately help the national side to achieve the same sort of results.

Sandwiched between the North West win and the North East defeat was the regional trial game between the North and the South and South West. If our dominance needed any more emphasizing, the 31 to 9 hammering we dished out that day was it. There was a seventeen-year-old lock called John Scott in the other team, but I wasn't in opposition to this young upstart because for the first time in a representative game I was stretching my legs at number eight.

The final England trial was held earlier than usual because of the international against the All Blacks. But there was no second-row or number eight spot for me; instead I was put on the flank ... well, anything was an improvement on touch judge! Also with me in the Rest fifteen was Gosforth full-back Brian Patrick, who was still at school. His wait for further honours was a long one – the 1981 England tour of Argentina.

I marked my card with a try that afternoon, just being tall enough to reach out of Alan Old's tackle to place the ball over the line with one hand. With Brian Patrick adding a couple of penalties and the conversion of that try, Gosforth provided all the Rest's points in a 12 point to 19 defeat.

The press reacted favourably to my positional switch and the majority had me in their England fifteen. Fortunately for England's rugby, none of them is allowed near a selection meeting, although it has been rumoured for many years that the best England selector was John Reason, then of the *Daily*, now of the *Sunday Telegraph*.

I was disappointed yet again. Also missing was Peter Dixon, the 1972 captain who had been unable to tour South Africa, His last game in the 1972 campaign was in Paris, where England suffered their heaviest-ever defeat drowning by 37 points to 12. But most people thought his demise was for reasons other than his ability as a player and captain: Peter was fairly uncompromising in his after-match speeches, something which is always guaranteed to put off the authorities.

That team selection heralded a troubled month or so for me. I was so desperate to be part of the England set-up, and this almost over-rode any desires I had for them to be successful without me. In a Jekyll and Hyde state, I outwardly supported a side that inwardly I was wanting to falter because then I'd be allowed my long-awaited chance.

I hadn't given up, but much of the early-season impetus had vanished. My problem would have been much worse if the rugby at Gosforth had not been so rewarding. I wasn't even requested to attend any of the squad sessions, so I assumed that I was further away from the team than generally thought. Why then had they wanted to take me to South Africa? I gave up searching for the answer to that; if they wanted me, they knew where to find me!

England were beaten by the All Blacks, and then fared even worse against the might of Wales down in Cardiff. Their next assignment was a trip to Dublin and I didn't envy them their task, as Ireland had only been beaten once at Lansdowne Road since 1967.

On the Sunday after the Welsh defeat, Kris and I were at home watching the television when there was a knock on the door. The caller was John Elders who asked the question that didn't need an answer: 'How do you fancy playing against Willie John McBride in a fortnight's time? I've just come from Bisham and you've got what you've been waiting for. Congratulations. I though you'd like to know before you read it in tomorrow's papers.'

At long last, I had made it. My first reaction was panic; it was time to put my money where my mouth was. Life has never been the same since. There were loads of 'good luck' wishes, and writers and reporters were suddenly very keen for my opinions. Everyone at Cramlington High School, where I'd been since September, was delighted; the kids, too, with their totally disarming honesty; asked, 'Do you really think you can cope with Willie John, sir?'

Well, if the truth be known, I wasn't sure. I might not be the raw-boned novice of the Ulster game several years earlier, but Willie John was now a legend and had his reputation to protect. Perhaps old age was getting to him. Keep talking, Roger, that's what you're good at!

My official invitation, engraved with the red rose, arrived on Tuesday complete with details of travel and dress arrangements. Because of the Irish 'troubles'. we had all been asked earlier in the season if anyone had objections to playing in Dublin. The 1972 championship had been disrupted when both Scotland and Wales refused to travel. That was a great pity because Wales won all their three matches, while Ireland had been successful in both away games and had high hopes of the Grand Slam. But the Ireland–Wales confrontation never took place and the championship table was incomplete.

Some papers said that my introduction was due to Peter Larter along with Sam Doble not wanting to visit Ireland. Even to this day, I am not sure whether I was selected on merit or not. Peter was in the RAF and, as such, might have been a target for terrorist attack. But Terry O'Connor stated at the time in the *Daily Mail* 'Sanders assures me that Larter was available for selection.' Even if I was second choice for the unavailable Peter Larter, I did not feel the honour was devalued in any way.

On the Thursday before the game, Kris dropped me at Newcastle station where I met John Elders. We travelled down together. I think Kris was glad to get rid of me. The game and very little else had occupied my thoughts since I

had heard the news. John and I linked with Peter Dixon at
Durham, who had been recalled. The match was also giving
another chance for Tony Jorden at full-back. The only other
new cap was a bubbling scrum-half from Sale who has
haunted my life ever since – Steve Smith.

After training at Stoop that afternoon, we flew over to
Dublin at about midday on Friday. The whole RFU committee was on the flight. Just as well it was a wide-bodied jet ... I
never realized there were so many of them! Normally they are
a species only to be found in twos and threes, but come the
Dublin or Paris weekends and they flock together from all
corners of England.

Our arrival at Dublin airport gave us some idea of the
security involved in the fixture and brought home the severity
of the political crisis. A motorcycle escort whisked us off to the
Shelborne Hotel, which had been cordoned off. Being confined to the hotel was a drag, especially as there were no
televisions in the rooms. One added attraction was that we
had vibrating beds, which were operated by placing 10p into a
slot machine. Not surprisingly, the novelty soon wore off.

That trip renewed my acquaintance with one of rugby's
great characters, Andy Ripley. Our paths had first crossed on
my maiden voyage to London with Gosforth. At the time, he
was being tipped for England honours. Even in those early
days with Rosslyn Park, he was immediately recognizable by
his long hair and off-beat sense of humour, which got worse
rather than better with age. With our interest in basketball
and canoeing, we struck up a rapport which remains to this
day. That particular day at Roehampton, Gosforth decided on
a long night and the milk train home. Andy and I must have
looked a strange sight as he drove me to the station in his
Mini, which was not designed for two giants. Andy had his
knees around his ears and, with my head sticking through the
roof, we brought some weird looks. Even in such a brief
meeting, Andy's lifestyle and free spirit made a great impression.

The confrontation with Willie John was now very close. Not
only was he the Irish captain, but this was his fiftieth cap; he
had already issued a public warning: 'It's tremendous to see

47

England coming over here. They'll get the welcome of all time, but after that they'll get no quarter.'

How right he was. Running onto the field in an England jersey for the first time was memorable enough, but this ovation was something special, even for the experienced players in the side. The whole of Lansdowne Road was on its feet to applaud us for ignoring the 'troubles'.

But the Irish hospitality ceased the minute the men in green emerged. The match passed in a blur, as though I was being swept along in a tide of action. All I could do was react as best I could when the ball came near me. With Chris Ralston and Andy Ripley in the line-out, John Pullin did his best to keep the throw-ins away from me and Willie John. I didn't know whether to be relieved or upset at being ignored, but John correctly reckoned I was having enough trouble with Willie John without worrying about the ball as well.

Ireland were well worth their 18 points to 9 victory and I sat rather dejectedly in the dressing room afterwards. When I confessed to Chris Ralston that I wanted to be part of a winning set-up, he responded; 'How do you think I feel? I was first capped in 1971 and I'm still waiting for my first win in the championship.'

His comments put my disappointment into perspective; at least I had survived my initiation, well the playing one anyway. After the dinner, Peter Dixon and I were taken out by Fergus Slattery and Kevin Mays. Where were the security forces when I needed their protection from the excesses of Dublin? All I can really remember is flopping into bed in the early hours somewhat the worse for wear ... like the game, it had all been a haze.

My ordeal was not yet over. On the flight back to Newcastle, Peter and I were nearing the recovery stage, but unfortunately came in contact with Bobby Robinson and Andy Bell, two dangerous Northumberland rugby men. Alcohol was the answer to our problem, they reckoned, and by the time we landed at Newcastle we were back to square one again.

With my first cap safely under my belt, the next job was to secure my place. I was still in for the next match, against France at Twickenham. Two more newcomers were added;

Peter Squires came in and Martin Cooper was made fly-half to try and solve the problems created by the injury to Alan Old, which had kept him out all season.

A brace of tries by the delighted David Duckham, his first for England for three years, were enough to see off the French. The fans celebrated England's first win in the championship to end a run of ten consecutive European defeats. The final opposition that season were the Scots – in their centenary year and one win away from their first Triple Crown since 1938. Ian McLauchlan's side was very optimistic; it had been five games since they had lost to England.

But grave doubts hung over the fitness of their inspiring leader, who had broken a leg during their Irish game only three weeks previously. As in the French game we established a 14 to nil lead, this time with tries from Peter Dixon (two) and Peter Squires. The Scots retaliated, but after they had closed the gap to one point, we moved ahead to 20 to 13 to dent their hopes yet again.

Pleasingly, one of Peter Dixon's tries came from a planned move. Working a 'peel' from a tap-down by Andy Ripley, Fran Cotton carried the move round the tail of the line-out. He popped the ball up to me and I took out Scotland's fly-half Colin Telfer before passing back inside to Peter Dixon. He picked the ball off his toes and his momentum carried him over, despite the attentions of three despairing Scottish tacklers. It sounds quite simple and normally worked well on the training field, but these moves seldom go so smoothly in the confusion of international rugby. It is a score I really cherish.

England's involvement in the Scottish centenary was not over. With Melrose, the originators of seven-a-side rugby, the Scottish Rugby Union came up with the inspired idea of holding a commemorative competition at Murrayfield. England were victorious that day and hold the title still; unfortunately, this invigorating exercise has yet to be repeated. One of the day's highlights, as I watched from the replacements' bench, was the sight of Andy Ripley leaving Mike Gibson trailing in his wake in the final. Mike Gibson was no slouch, even by international standards, but such was Andy's prowess that the Irishman could make no impression on the distance between them.

Later that day I was approached by someone I had seen at some of Gosforth's recent matches and who had spoken to me briefly on a couple of occasions. Now, at the North British, he commiserated with me about not getting a game and wondered if I would like to have a drink in the bar with a friend of his. This was, in fact, my first encounter with rugby league and their persuasive ways. The pair were the chairman and secretary of Wigan; they thought I had what it takes to make it in rugby league. Their offer was tempting, but life was enjoyable in the north east; Kris and I had settled in a house in the Westhorpe area of Newcastle and, while the money was not rolling in, we had enough to get by. Still, they could have made me an offer to which I wouldn't have said no.

The sum offered was £12,000, not all payable at once and subject to appearances and representative games. A lot could have gone wrong and I might have found I had taken the irrevocable step for peanuts. So I said no; it was then up to them to show that they really wanted me. Considering the back problems that affected me over the next few years, it was just as well I stayed with the union code.

Coincidentally, two of England's winning seven that day were to sign away their amateur status and never looked back. Keith Fielding became one of rugby league's legendary try-scorers, with Salford, and, recently, one of the more successful competitors on 'Superstars'. Hooker John Gray, after a slow start, found fame and fortune in Australia. When we bumped into him during England's 1975 tour there, he was leading the life of a film star.

If I had been guaranteed that sort of success, then I might have signed, but I've never had any regrets. Refusing their offers also enabled me to accept the invitation of one of the most famous amateur organizations in the world, the Barbarians, to join their Easter tour of south Wales. No sport anywhere can offer a more enjoyable experience, although my initial reaction was one of caution when I arrived at the hotel.

'Ah, you must be Utling.' Nice try; what had I let myself in for? But the weekend turned out to be marvellous and the club's secretary and unpaid liaison officer between players and committee, Geoffrey Windsor Lewis, has become a true friend over the years.

The Barbarians were riding high at the time. Their classic encounter with Ian Kirkpatrick's All Blacks in January had helped to erase most of the unhappy memories of that tour. This Easter, the president Brigadier Glyn Hughes, was celebrating the sixtieth year of his connection with the Barbarians (his first game with them had been against Penarth in 1913). As a tribute to his long service, the Barbarians ran up sixty points in the final match against Newport. My appearances had been in the games against Cardiff and Swansea; we ended the short visit with four wins out of four.

Easter Sunday is spent demonstrating the art of coarse golf at the Glamorgan Country Club, at Penarth. Some of our players would be more appropriately equipped with picks and shovels. Traditionally, the club members stay away for fear of seeing what is happening to their beautiful course.

John Spencer's foursome left the clubhouse to the strains of 'Hi, ho, hi, ho,' while Robin Challis was looking for a trolley or caddie to carry his crate of Guinness. We used Tom David as our mark while making our drives from the second tee; Tom stood at the top of the hill and pointed the way to the flag. Unfortunately, someone (who hasn't shown such accuracy since) drilled the ball into the small of Tom's back; luckily they breed them tough in Pontypridd.

The stiffest ordeal of the whole tour had come the previous night when the newcomers to the Barbarians are required to provide the cabaret. Neither Tom Jones nor Frank Sinatra would have broken out in a cold sweat if they had heard my rendition of 'Wor Geordie's lost his penka' a song of great social significance up north; I don't know whose embarrassment was greater, mine or the audience's. The evening was saved by a ventriloquist act from Steve Smith and Fran Cotton, although the dialogue would have never got past the censor.

That weekend was obviously going to be in stark contrast with England's proposed summer tour of Argentina. The destination did not fill me with a great sense of excitement and, when the tour was cancelled because of terrorist threats, I felt no tremendous sense of loss.

In double quick time, the RFU arranged a five match tour of Fiji and New Zealand. The schedule was frightening, to say the least; the international in Fiji, followed by three hard provincial games in New Zealand rounded off with a test against the All Blacks. But, however forbidding the opposition might be, a chance to visit one of the great rugby nations was a marvellous opportunity for me.

From an historical point of view, the countries to travel to are New Zealand and South Africa, although there wasn't a lot wrong with Fiji. The island was such a warm and friendly place that it should have been tagged on to the end of the tour, and not been our starting-point. The carnival atmosphere created some hilarious moments – such as Steve Smith being attacked by frogs on the training field. David Duckham's sole purpose on the trip seemed to be to buy up half of Suva. We presented Jan Webster with a traditional grass skirt on his birthday. He wore it, too; he had to – we'd taken his shorts. The laughing quickly stopped in our game with the islanders. This bunch of talented ball-runners gave us a hell of a fright, and we clinched the narrowest of victories when Peter Squires's last-minute try edged us 13 points to 12 ahead and saved face for England. But, that apart, those five days in Fiji were like a holiday and no preparation at all for what was to follow in New Zealand.

The mud of New Plymouth was the scene of our opening game in New Zealand. Taranaki were much more adaptable to the conditions; the rain poured throughout and sun-drenched Fiji seemed a million miles away. We floundered badly and Taranaki well deserved their 6–3 victory. After I had played lock against Fiji and been rested against Taranaki the selectors decided to experiment, and put me at number eight against Wellington, with Steve Smith at scrum-half. Andy Leslie, later to captain New Zealand, led the home side, which also included a young student on the flank by the name of Graham Mourie.

Steve and I had a disastrous day, mainly due to my inexperience in the number eight position at representative level.

Wellington led 21 to 3 at the interval and, although we recovered some ground, we had left ourselves with too much to do and lost 16 to 25. Graham Mourie, with a well-taken try, had shown enough nice touches to mark him down as one to watch in the future.

The bad publicity about violence in Canterbury's games against the 1966 and 1971 Lions rather distracted us from our task. I was back at lock, but the 12 to 19 defeat meant we had lost all our provincial games. With that record, we were written off by the New Zealand press as no-hopers. It wasn't so much a question of who would win, but by how many. We spent the week before the test at the beautiful Bay of Islands so as to get some peace and quiet before our ordeal. Although our results suggested that beating the All Blacks on their home ground was an impossible task, none of the players had given up the fight; all believed that the impossible was possible.

That Wellington experiment with me at number eight had cost Steve Smith the scrum-half berth, which went to Jan Webster. Steve has never really forgiven me for leaving his international career in tatters, especially as I found a place in the test team in the second-row. I suppose this will have to do as a public apology!

When we travelled to Auckland a couple of days before the test, some people were even surprised that we had bothered to appear. But as John Pullin had said at the after-match dinner following the Irish game; 'We might not be much good, but we do at least turn up.'

My room-mate was Christopher Wayne Ralston; we were to share many times before he left the international scene in 1975. His behaviour followed a rigid pattern; cigarette last thing at night *and* first thing in the morning. That I didn't mind too much ... it was when he started on the cigars that I really objected.

The changing rooms at Eden Park must be among the most miserable and cold in the world. It was almost a relief to get onto the park to face the All Blacks. New Zealand decided to use the wind advantage, but could not have been happy with the 10 points to 6 lead at the interval. In the second half, finding reserves of strength and character that many doubted were even there, England surged back to take the lead. And when the final whistle went, we were still in front. Our 16 points to 10 success meant we had become the first home country ever to win in New Zealand. That win, coupled with the South African victory the year before, was all the more amazing because of the desperately poor form we showed when we were at home. Jan Webster played the game of his life and many reckon his performance at scrum-half that day one of the finest they have ever seen. John Watkins was another who shone, but my most vivid memory is of Fran Cotton bursting down the left-hand touch-line late into the game. If this was not presumptuous enough on its own, he threw a couple of cheeky dummies which completely hood-winked the opposition and brought a huge roar of approval from the crowd. For a visiting prop to commit such a crime in New Zealand only served to emphasize our superiority.

For some reason or another, I was never able to get into the game and find it difficult to describe. The scenes of jubilation and celebration in the dressing room seemed divorced from my feelings. My form on the tour had disappointed me and, anyway, I never react to rugby achievements immediately. That certainly was not true of some of the others. John Watkins was in tears and everyone else seemed cock-a-hoop, especially Sandy Sanders, the manager. I just gazed at these goings on and wondered what all the fuss was about. As ever, alcohol brought its relief and I slowly felt myself becoming one of the party again.

The New Zealand press were left with little choice but to eat their own words and acclaim our triumph. Many started by slating their own players. One journalist whom I've always respected, Terry McLean, had a fairer verdict. 'The All Blacks were hammered, outfought forward. And this, I tell you, is no fairy story. New Zealand, moreover, were out-thought in general tactics.' As I had missed South Africa, I couldn't compare the two famous victories, but John Pullin, captain in both matches, could. 'An even better win than the one over the Springboks,' was how he described it. Who was I to disagree?

Had it really been a year since I had had to cry off from that England tour? So much had happened since. Again, England were flying home heroes; this time I was with them!

4

South Africa Demolished

John Pullin wasn't finished making winning speeches. The arrival of Australia in the autumn of 1973 gave England the chance of completing the hat-trick over all three major rugby-playing countries in the southern hemisphere. I missed the Northern Counties match against the tourists because it was played on the Tuesday before the England international. Our hopes were certainly given a boost when the North triumphed 16 to 13. The Australian match proved the easiest of our trio of wins. A try from Tony Neary helped us to a 7 nil lead and we scored two more tries in the second half to emerge fairly comfortable winners by 20 points to 3. In such a period of depressing results at home, this achievement of beating South Africa, New Zealand and Australia was an amazing feat; it only served, though, to confuse our supporters as to why we couldn't turn such form on at home.

The North figured strongly in the national trials and everybody was optimistic as we set off to Murrayfield for the opening clash of the season. During the Friday work-out at North Berwick, something cropped up that was to affect my rugby for the rest of my career. As I bent down to pick up a rolling ball, I strained a back muscle. It did not seem that serious at the time and Nigel Horton was sent for only as a precautionary measure. I was not the only casualty: Steve Smith had pulled a hamstring and Jan Webster was recalled. I didn't make the match and had to watch the proceedings from the stand. In a topsy-turvy game, Peter Rossborough looked to have won the Calcutta Cup for England when he dropped a magnificent goal with three minutes to go.

But the season started to go wrong when in the dying

minute David Duckham was caught off-side. From forty yards and with the final kick of the afternoon, Andy Irvine became the hero of the Scots as his penalty kick flew over to give the home side a 16 points to 14 victory.

I nearly missed the Irish game a fortnight later when I aggravated the back injury by, of all things, leaning forward to switch on the television. I was kept out of Gosforth's cup defeat by Coventry by this trouble but it cleared up sufficiently to allow me to play at Twickenham.

I need not have bothered really. The 26 points to 21 score line in Ireland's favour may sound close, but they led 26 to 9 at one stage and scored four times to one; our only means of salvation lay in the boot of Alan Old, who rattled up 17 points.

With the matches against France, in Paris, and Wales to come, this start did not exactly overwhelm us with confidence and the mood wasn't that optimistic as we crossed the Channel. But, I found, as I had done with England Schools a few years earlier, that visiting France was exhilarating. After training in snow in Paris we travelled to Versailles to spend the traditional Friday night; the setting is marvellous and I have always enjoyed the French attitude to life in general.

Chris Ralston and I were a fairly regular partnership in the second row at this time and usually shared a room. We had first met on the 1971 Far East tour as the young pretenders to the spots occupied by Dave Watt and Peter Larter. With his long hair and incredible consumption of cigarettes, Chris hardly cut the figure of the traditional rugby player. I always remember him in Sri Lanka lying on the bed with only the glow of his cigarettes regularly visible counterpointed by the growling smoker's cough. Chris always seemed to shamble around rather than run.

In the line-out, however, he reigned supreme and it was only when you packed down alongside him that you realised just how bulky he was. The lads in the side always used to describe us as the ugliest second row in the business; we consoled ourselves with the fact that, although we did not have classic good looks, we conveyed a certain amount of admirable rugged qualities.

57

The snow was still about on Saturday morning as we prepared for the trip to Paris, our path through the heavy traffic being cut like a knife through butter by the boys in blue on bikes. The snow was missing from the Parc des Princes pitch, which was crisp and firm.

Our record in Paris was hardly convincing and in the last visit there Peter Dixon's side had been hammered 37 to 12. However, we found a lot of our pride that day and held our heads high with a 12 all draw. We trailed by 12 points to 3, all the French points having come from Jean-Pierre Romeu, who scored a try, conversion, penalty and dropped goal; then we gave David Duckham a rare chance to show his paces as he raced the thirty five yards to the corner. Alan Old's conversion tied the scores with twenty minutes to go, and that is how it remained at the finish. The result made the evening all the more enjoyable. Rather the worse for wear, we ended up at the Crazy Horse; that was an eye-opening experience – they only had the Winter Gardens in Blackpool!

All these celebrations left Sunday morning rather confused and there was quite a delay in leaving, for which perhaps unfairly Colonel Morgan was blamed. There was more chaos at the airport, but eventually we were called for our flight by the Pakistan International Airlines staff. On the plane we discovered that Alan Old and Tony Jorden had been left behind. They flew out an hour later.

At Heathrow, John Elders, Peter Dixon and I were due to fly to Newcastle. John went to phone his wife. He reappeared a few minutes later and asked if I had been in touch with Kris. He said he thought I should. The plane we were supposed to catch had crashed on its ascent from Paris. Radio reports said there were a lot of white shirts in the wreckage, which were believed to have belonged to the national side.

Kris sounded so relieved to hear my voice. Had it not been for that late start, we would have been on that DC 10. She hadn't heard the news from the radio, but my best man Mick Mahoney had rung her and asked in a roundabout way if she had heard from me. When she replied no, he told her the news before coming round with his wife Lucia to keep her company. That had been a few hours ago.

There was some discussion now about whether we should fly back to Newcastle or not; we were too tired to bother going to King's Cross to take a train.

It was only during the following week that the magnitude of the crash – over 350 people killed – hit me. Almost the whole playing strength of the Bury St Edmunds club was wiped out. The crash hit me the hardest when I rang up Adidas for another pair of boots on Monday. While in Paris, I had had breakfast on the Saturday morning with John Cooper, the Olympic hurdler who was now working with Adidas public relations and looking after competitors in the sports in which the company was involved. I mentioned to John that my boots were on the way out, so he gave me his number and said to call and he'd sort it out. When I called, I was told that he would not be coming in. When I said that I had been asked to ring this number, the receptionist broke down crying and said that John had been a passenger on the DC10 which crashed.

I made my commiserations and put the phone down. Suddenly, and rather selfishly I offered a silent prayer that fate had saved me from such a death.

Later in the season we played a special international against the French for the dependants of those killed. Before that we finished our campaign against Wales at Twickenham. Despite complaints from the visitors of bad refereeing, we snatched a rare win against the red dragon. The first incident came when John West decided that Peter Squires had just prevented J.J. Williams from touching down for a try. The second, and more important, was when Phil Bennett broke clear through, but was brought back by the referee for a penalty to Wales, who would surely have preferred the advantage. But we deserved our luck after suffering from several bad bounces over the years.

That game was the only time in an international when I have inflicted serious damage to another player, albeit unintentionally. My victim was Ian Robinson, a nice man off the field who turned into a snarling, vicious animal when he pulled on a rugby jersey. When Wales won a line-out ball, I broke through to try to prevent distribution, someone was holding me back. Instinctively, I swung my arm back fiercely, made contact with something and was allowed to carry on my way. I kept moving because I thought retribution would be at hand. Eventually, I got caught in a ruck and waited for something to hit me somewhere. The whistle went and I cautiously got to my feet to see the referee run back to attend Ian Robinson, who was led from the field suffering from a broken jaw. The action was not premeditated on my part and was just a reaction to a certain situation.

The individual countries were all combined as British rugby prepared to visit South Africa. My showing in the last two internationals against France and Wales had boosted my chances, but I still could not quite see myself making it as one of the four locks. Willie John McBride seemed the obvious choice as captain, so was certain to take on the test spots. He needed a top line-out jumper as a partner and so Chris Ralston and Delme Thomas seemed the most obvious contenders, with one or both of the Scottish pair – Alastair McHarg and Gordon Brown – likely to be included. I considered myself very much among the also-rans, but had returned my availability slip in extra quick time.

Then lo and behold, there was my name when the thirty players were announced. My second-row companions were Willie John (captain), Chris Ralston and Gordon Brown. The surprise omission, I felt, was Big Al McHarg, who had been in storming form for Scotland against France on the day that we beat Wales. Not only was he excellent in the line-out but he had scored a try; everybody thought he had booked his seat on the plane. A lot of people argued that the wayward Scot was something of a joke figure and that his unorthodoxy was no example for the aspiring youngster. But his commitment in the line-out was first-class and he formed a fearful pairing with Gordon Brown.

There were several of my England colleagues in the party, although the surprise for most of us was that John Pullin was not included as one of the two hookers. Other England players in the pack were Fran Cotton, Mickey Burton, and Tony Neary. With Peter Squires declining to tour because of cricket commitments, and David Duckham also unavailable, our contingent in the back line was restricted to Geoff Evans and Alan Old.

I felt very honoured to be included among so many famous names and the trip was more than I had expected after just over a year of international rugby. It is a tour I wouldn't have missed for the world; our performance out there prompted as much media coverage as any overseas tour from Britain.

Coach Syd Millar described our task when we assembled in London at the Britannia Hotel. 'For the benefit of you newcomers, I will explain what three months away on tour is like. We have twenty-two games to look forward to and something in the region of seventy training sessions to take part in. For most of you this is the pinnacle of your careers and your only chance to play an amateur game on a professional basis. We cannot fail if everybody pulls their weight; anything less is a waste of time. This tour is a personal challenge to all of you.'

We were also informed about the apartheid laws and had already faced a hostile attitude from those not wanting us to visit South Africa. We had all received literature through the post from Peter Hain and his colleagues. One of my fellow teachers at Cramlington, a woman, felt I ought to withdraw. I explained, rather smugly perhaps, that I wanted to see for myself. The Northumberland education authority had given me leave of absence with pay; now I only had myself to worry about for three months. Before we left, I shared a room with Gordon Brown, a veteran of the 1971 tour, and I was quickly comforted by his complete confidence in our adventure.

My first problem was being kitted out. Any blazer that covered my arms came only halfway up my back; eventually, Albert Agar, the then secretary of the Four Home Unions' tours committee, took J.P.R. Williams, another odd-shaped being, and myself to Lillywhites, where we at last found something to fit.

The mood of the tour was established before we left when choirmaster Gordon Brown persuaded Billy Steele to sing 'Oh Flower of Scotland,' a song that was to play an important part in the tour, though not through any nationalist feeling from North of the border.

After losing Bobby Windsor off the plane with gastro-enteritis, we were greeted by the legendary figure of Dr Danie Craven. He welcomed us warmly and thanked us for coming.

The comedians of the tour quickly emerged. Bobby Windsor and Mickey Burton competed for top spot, while Andy Ripley had a style all of his own and also carried a portable tape-recorder. 'Band on the Run' will even today produce a faraway look in the eye of the 1974 Lions. Trying to get Andy properly dressed for the many functions was a major task and the management seldom achieved it. Andy's trademark became the kaffir sandals that I think he picked up on the England tour in 1972; they were made out of old rubber tyres and the big man chalked up a few miles in his travels through South Africa.

For my own part, I was just happy to be there and to fit in any way I could. It seemed early on as if I would play second string to the top second-row pairing of Willie John and either Gordon Brown or Chris Ralston. The formation of the back row was interesting. Mervyn Davies had had a poor inter-national season by his high standards; the early front-funners appeared to be Tony Neary, Andy Ripley and Tom David, who were selected in the initial senior side.

Even on the way to that first game against Western Province there was an incident which demonstrated the attitude of some of the whites towards the blacks. A car of whites in front of us passed a couple of natives, one of whom was pushing a bike as they walked along the road. As the car passed them, a hand came out carrying a can which was thrown, hitting one of the walkers, much to the great delight of the car passengers. A sickening spectacle.

It wasn't long before Gordon Brown was stretching his long frame for the first try of the tour. This started him off on a try-scoring orgy of eight for the visit (he never scored one in his thirty Scotland internationals). The lads put in a promising performance in the opening game and ran out comfortable winners.

The rest of us had our chance the following Saturday against South West Africa, led by the legendary Jan Ellis.

This time we struggled and were behind three times before coming through to win by 23 points to 16. With initial impressions so important, the players selected for the first game had gained an obvious advantage and some of us were worried that we might have been labelled 'Dirt Trackers' – the Wednesday side – so early on.

From there we travelled to Cape Town, where we learned that the British Government had ordered that we weren't to be entertained at the embassy and that the embassy staff were barred from seeing us play. It wasn't very pleasant being abandoned by your own country – officially, that is – but missing out on many of those rather formal parties was not a great blow.

Syd Millar really put us through some torrid scrummaging before meeting Boland in the third game. It was mainly the side that had played Western Province which was given the nod and I was back on the replacements' bench. My versatility made me an obvious contender for a place there and I was to spend a large part of my tour watching, ready to join the action. I didn't mind because it kept me involved ... and sometimes I got onto the field. I did against Boland when Tommy David pulled a hamstring and I played the final twenty minutes on the flank, a position where some people were saying I might be of more use against the South Africans.

I was back to partner Gordon Brown in the game against Eastern Province, a match which degenerated into something of a running brawl. At one line-out, Mickey Burton took a swing at one of their players and down he went. Running across the field, I rather naively inquired what was going on.

'Those blokes are taking liberties and they've got to be stopped.'

'But, let's play rugby,' I replied, to which Mickey almost fell over laughing.

Fortunately, we had a good mixture of people with expertise in both areas of rugby, i.e. the ball and self-defence. As a pointer for the rest of the tour, this game provided the opposition with the irrefutable fact that, although we were there to play rugby, if they wanted to take us on physically, then we had the ability to defend ourselves.

In fact the Sunday morning was to prove a bigger ordeal than anything we met on the rugby field. The Eastern Province officials organized a fishing trip for about ten of us and, with plenty of beer and food on the boat, we set off. We hadn't even left the harbour before Billy Steele was heaving over the side and being taunted unmercifully by Gareth Edwards. His turn was to come. Once the boat had been anchored and was bobbing around, the real trouble began.

Edwards, the taunter, joined me at the bow of the boat and, having nearly lost our dentures in the opening bout of sea-sickness, we put them in our pockets for the rest of the day. The skipper took no notice of our pleadings to return to harbour. Our helplessness was not relieved by the sight of Mickey Burton and Mervyn Davies eating and drinking at will and giving a running commentary on the various catastrophes that were taking place around the edge of the boat. I even contemplated letting myself slip between the waves just to escape.

As I'd done in London before we left, I shared with Gordon Brown in Port Elizabeth. Fortunately, it was my last firsthand evidence of 'Broonie's' snoring habits. I can only compare them to Popeye, with drawers opening and curtains blowing inwards as he inhaled and the drawers banging shut and the curtain flying through the window as the air thundered out again.

An unpleasant experience for many of the guys were our several trips on the Second World War Dakotas. For Messrs McBride, Windsor, McKinney and Ralston, eyes were fixed straight ahead for both landing and take-off. The comments from the lads who felt safe were not designed to ease their condition.

The first test was approaching and everybody was keen to play against Western Province, the last Saturday game before the international. I hadn't played, but many of us felt slightly hopeful again when the side struggled to win by 17 points to 8 and it was obvious that changes would be made. I was selected on the flank for the mid-week game against Proteas, with Mervyn Davies and Fergus Slattery for company in the back row. During the game we lost Alan Old to a vicious late tackle, just when he looked a certainty for the test. It was the end of his tour, a tragedy because he was showing the selectors back home what a talent he was.

The following morning we all gathered in the team-room to hear whether or not we had made the test side. And, with very little opportunity to see if I was up to the job, I was in on the flank, as the back row which had played against the Proteas was selected. These announcements can be very embarrassing; you're either deliriously happy or very disappointed, even upset. Tony Neary felt aggrieved and said as much to the management. I was surprised to have kept someone of his class and ability out of the side, but he told me not to be so daft. The pack was made up of a pair from each of the four countries – Willie John and Fergus from Ireland, 'Mouse' and Gordon Brown from Scotland, Mervyn and Bobby Windsor (Wales) and Fran and myself from England. Wales also provided Gareth Edwards and Phil Bennett at half-back, with J.J.Williams on the wing and J.P.R. Williams at full-back. Billy Steele was on the other wing and the centres were Dick Milliken and Ian McGeechan.

On the Thursday before the international, we trained at Stellenbosch University and had one of our best-ever sessions. That famous team photograph, taken after a hard slog, is my favourite and helps to explain why we beat the Springboks. Friday was a rest day and King Kipper (Fran) and I went for a walk after dinner, talking of home but looking forward to tomorrow.

The tension was obvious as we entered the team-room on Saturday for our pre-match talk. There, at the head, was Willie John, impassively smoking his pipe, only making a faint acknowledgement as people came in. For twenty minutes there was silence as everyone prepared inwardly for the task at hand. Then the great man broke the silence. 'There is no escape, we must go on.' Newlands was wet and boggy, with the warm-up games chewing up the turf; but we were concerned with the opposition not the environment. Early on I arrived at a breakdown just as the ball was produced on our side; I continued the attack, took on one of the defenders and then laid the ball back efficiently. After that I concentrated on

65

my job with increased confidence. At half-time the score was 3 points all, but we had the wind behind us and our pack was in control, with Gareth Edwards and Phil Bennett tying up the Springboks with their superb tactical kicking.

The final score of 12 points to 3 in our favour may not sound conclusive, but we had set our standard for the rest of the series and South Africa was going to have to improve considerably to make a contest of the series. Suddenly, after regarding myself as the four choice lock, here I was an important part of the successful test team. Playing me on the flank after so little experience was a tremendous risk; no one was more aware of this than I was. Now, with such an historic victory· behind us, I felt I could play anywhere.

Around this time, I heard the news that Kris was pregnant; it was difficult to appreciate in my privileged environment, where almost everything was done for me, that I was going to ·have to be responsible for a family of three after I returned.

It was a relief to get out of Cape Town in the end; the weather had been terrible and we wanted the sun on our backs again. Almost on arrival in Johannesburg I felt run down and was sent to bed by Syd. For this part of the tour I had the great honour of sharing a room with the one and only G.O. Edwards. The phone never stopped ringing and I had to act as his personal secretary, vetting the calls and seeing whether the scrum-half was officially in or not. As we were to play Transvaal the following day, I was relieved when Gareth went off for a round of golf. I needed the rest before such a big game.

My slumbers were interrupted by a banging at the door. Gareth's golf had been followed by a lot of wine during a meal and I found him in rather a dishevelled state. He apologized for disturbing me the night before a big game and slumped into bed. I had just dropped off again, when there was obvious distress sounds from Gareth's bed; I rushed up and helped him to the toilet. More apologies. 'What a room-mate you are! Hey, let me go to another room – you've got a big game tomorrow.' The disturbances and the apologies continued for an hour or so before Gareth eventually crashed out. I couldn't get back to sleep for ages.

The great man was looking much the worse for wear the next morning and there were more gushing thank-yous for looking after him, for taking his teeth out and for putting a rubbish bin by his bed. Nevertheless, the all-England back row of Neary, Ripley and Uttley helped the Lions to a 23 points to 15 victory over Transvaal.

Then we moved up Pretoria for the second test. Pretoria is a real Afrikaner stronghold and the interest since our first test win had been phenomenal. By now we had settled into some sort of a routine. My daily routine was breakfast, followed by training, and then back to the hotel for a light lunch. The afternoons were either spent sleeping or writing home or reading or playing the recorder which I had bought myself in Pretoria (I didn't see much of my room-mate Billy Steele during this period). By the end of the tour, I had built up a little repertoire on this instrument, though nobody seemed to want to hear it.

We arrived at the ground for the second test midway through our rendition of 'Flower of Scotland', but nobody moved until we had finished; team spirit was perfect. The Springboks had made many changes and brought in the powerful kicking fly-half Gerald Bosch as the man to solve their problems. But he, like the rest of his side, was swept aside as the Lions surpassed their performance of the first game. Again, Gareth and Phil were magnificent at half-back as we ran in five tries to bury the Springboks by 28 points to 9; South African rugby had never known anything like this. Two of the tries came from J.J. Williams, but the highlight of the day was a fifty-yard side-stepping effort from Phil Bennett; two up with two to play – I doubted if the home side could recover from this thrashing.

I had now played six games on the trot, two of them tests, and I was exhausted; all I wanted to do was rest, my play was on the verge of becoming stale. We journeyed to the Kruger Game Park for a rest; the Lions amongst the lions, you may say. By this stage of the tour, they looked far more impressive than we did.

Andy Irvine came in on the wing for Billy Steele in the third test. That was the only change, but the South Africans had

67

again made wholesale changes and their performance in the first half was a great improvement. Just before the interval, with the teams tied at 3 points all, Gordon Brown stole a Springbok throw near the front of the line-out and dived over. It was his eighth try of the tour and set the Lions on the road to another thundering victory. J.J. Williams again added a couple of tries and we had triumphed by 26 points to 9. The series was ours and for Willie John, a loser there in 1962 and 1968, the boot was now on the other foot. With the job finished, I wanted to go home and see Kris, who was by now three months pregnant, but there was a fortnight of the tour left, including the fourth test.

On the way back to East London our plane had to turn back after a sea bird had strayed into one of the turbines just after take-off. This was the final straw as far as the non-flyers were concerned and they departed by road, on four wheels.

In the run-in to the final test, there was the much publicized incident between J.P.R. Williams and Tommy Bedford as we trounced Natal in injury time. We completed our winning way in provincial matches by beating Eastern Transvaal by 33 points to 10.

I was pleased when the team for the final test was announced and Chris Ralston came in at lock for the injured Gordon Brown, who had broken his hand in the third test. I think that all our plans and thoughts for returning home were evident in our performance at Johannesburg. Errors crept into our play that had not been seen before. We got off to a good start when referee Max Baise awarded me a try, but I have to be honest and say that their winger Chris Pope was easily there first and photographic evidence seemed to bear that out. Shortly after, Fran knocked lumps out of my knee when I was struck at the bottom of a ruck; my interest began to wane from then on. My final playing memory of the tour is the tremendous surge of pride and self-sacrifice as everyone pulled out their last drop of energy to try to produce a winning score. There was great frustration when Fergus Slattery had his late try disallowed, although that probably cancelled out my try. So the final result was a 13–13 draw; at least we had maintained our unbeaten record in twenty-two games. Including two games as replacement, I had only missed six matches and had made the most appearances on the trip.

Suddenly it was all over; we had achieved the ultimate, and what a satisfying experience that was. On a personal level, the tour couldn't have gone better, as my prospects had seemed limited at the start, to say the least. Looking back, I regarded those three months in South Africa as the pinnacle of my career – I have never been fitter, so free of injury, and I have never played such consistently high standard rugby.

We arrived home to a hero's welcome; even the politicians who had abandoned us were there to extend the hand of friendship. This somewhat unprincipled gesture was not ignored by the players, but we saw it for what it was worth – not a lot. Kris was at the airport to meet me, although she was rather tired after the journey down from Newcastle. Then as she was getting on the bus to go to a reception, she fell backwards over a bag. This episode, coupled with the long day and four-hour wait at Heathrow to fly back home made her start to haemorrhage. The outcome was that she lost the baby; so I did not have the happiest of returns to the old country.

5

War in Australia

I should have known better than to take notice of the promising signs from the Lions tour that suggested that England might be coming out of the international wilderness. England's squad was, however, as good as anybody else's, except perhaps that of Wales. We had eight forwards available with experience from the 1971 and 1974 Lions visits. John Burgess, at last, was being given his chance of coaching the national team.

On a personal level, South Africa was my coming-of-age party, as far as rugby was concerned. I was now prepared, physically and mentally, to play top-class rugby. All the sunshine and exercise had boosted my weight from $15\frac{1}{2}$ stone to 16 stone 4 pounds ... no excess, just lean meat. Mentally, too, my attitude had hardened. This was noticed back home, by some people quicker than others. Playing for Northumberland against Cumberland and Westmoreland, one P.J. Dixon was up to his usual tricks in the line-out. In the past, I would probably have put up with this behaviour, but the experiences of South Africa had left me with a fairly low tolerance level. Peter tried one antic too many and I caught him round the face with a backhander. The look of surprise on his face was a treat and for a while, albeit briefly, he behaved himself.

Further memories of South Africa were rekindled with the visit of New Zealand to help the Irish celebrate their centenary. The All Blacks were also to play a Welsh fifteen at Cardiff midweek and finish their tour with a game against the Barbarians at Twickenham. As a tribute to our success and domination over the Springboks, the Barbarians picked the Lions test pack.

Although linking up with the lads again was enjoyable, the reunion was something of an anti-climax for me. The old sparkle was not there and we all knew that something was missing that had nothing to do with our playing ability. The truth became apparent that what we had created in South Africa over three months was something special and could not be turned on and off like a tap for eighty minutes for a one-off like this. Our mass selection brought protests that our presence would turn what was meant to be a spectacle into a test match. Many hoped for a repeat of that classic 1973 encounter between the two teams at Cardiff. But that, too, was a rare day and not likely to come round very often.

The 1974 All Blacks schedule was gruelling, especially in that final week then they had to play Ireland, Wales and the Barbarians. The game between a Welsh fifteen and New Zealand was not an official test, but who were they kidding? The pair have been at each other's throats for the whole of the century and this game was not going to be played any differently. But the All Blacks arrived at Twickenham with only us between them and a completely successful tour. We halted their charge by drawing 13 all and if Andy Irvine had converted Mervyn Davies's late try we would have won ... but that would have been a complete injustice. In fact, we were lucky to draw and the match was not a patch on the 1973 thriller.

In consequence, the press gave us a bit of a pasting. And, unfairly, on the evidence of this one showing they tried to devalue our efforts and achievements in South Africa. It seemed there was no pleasing people; we were castigated for not producing a traditional Barbarians performance and criticized for not bulldozing our path at Twickenham in the same way we had done against the Springboks. Heads they win, tails we lose! Andy Leslie, the All Blacks captain for whom I have tremendous respect, summed up our predicament. 'The 70,000 crowd went to Twickenham to see the Lions of South Africa fame, where they did not play Barbarians style football.'

While this game was a brief reminder of a unique experience, getting England back on the winning trail was the immediate aim. The build-up to the championship began with the North's regional game against the Midlands at Heading-ley. The day was memorable for two reasons. The first was that we turned a 3 points to 13 half-time deficit into a 28 to 13 victory, leaving John Burgess with a huge contented grin. The other was a senseless act of thuggery for which there was no justification or excuse. Captaining the Midlands side was Nigel Horton, and he set his players no example as he put his boot into Peter Dixons's face. Peter was trapped on the deck with his head exposed, and there was no escape as Nigel, an enigmatic figure in English rugby, drove into the scrum. It was a disappointing display from a talented player. The wound around Peter's nose needed twenty-two stitches and was a cold-blooded, calculated act, which flaunted rugby's self-imposed discipline. Without that self-discipline, the game quickly degenerates into war.

The only thing worse than premeditated violence by an individual is when such an approach is a matter of team policy and planning. I was to experience that sort of behaviour at first hand in Australia the following summer.

Fran Cotton took over as captain from John Pullin and hopes were high as we ventured to Dublin for our opening international. The result, and the subsequent panic by the selectors, had a shattering effect on the future performances of the national team and on the confidence of the players for several years. Luckily, I was absent from this disaster. Having joined the side on Thursday, my back went while I was eating lunch and I had to withdraw. I had been suffering from cold and I was gradually to find that any weakening illness would leave me more susceptible to back trouble.

In my place came a youngster who used to have to drop out of the first fifteen at Fylde when I came home from Ponteland during the college holidays. He has since become quite well known in rugby circles – William Blackledge Beaumont. His progress to the first cap was pretty startling because earlier in the season he was to be found on the replacements' bench when the England under twenty-three team played Tonga. Our paths first crossed, or rather came together, when we were partnered in the second row for that trial game at

Headingley earlier in the season. Our backgrounds were similar, especially with the Fylde connection, and as we were sharing a room on the Friday night we got talking of old times. I was rather embarrassed to discover he had felt some resentment at this college big-shot and great white hope waltzing straight into the side at his expense. Understandably, too.

Looking ahead to the trial, Bill asked me what it was like in the big time. Suddenly, for the first time, it dawned on me that I was no longer a newcomer to the international scene; instead, I was an experienced player to whom others were looking for guidance.

It had only been a few months since I was seeking help from Willie John, 'Mouse' and Mervyn. I explained to Bill that, with Chris Ralston and Andy Ripley in the side, my line-out duties had been limited, so I was able to concentrate on my scrummaging. My handling was good and I was able to operate like an extra loose-forward. This gave my game an all-round edge, so I gained the reputation of being able to play lock, number eight or flanker. Some people may have accused me of being jack of all positions and master of none, but I felt that my versatility gave me three chances of being selected.

My advice to Bill, from my 'vast' experience, was to concentrate on the scrum first, the line-out second, and anything after that would be a bonus. And it has been his complete and honest endeavour in these departments that has made him one of the most respected forwards in the world today. But, although he may not have liked my occasional performances for Fylde in the old days, I have done my best to further his career ever since ... indirectly, of course. With an almost impeccable sense of timing, Bill seems to have been the player to take advantage of my many misfortunes in the seventies. That was not his fault, of course, and he had made the most of his opportunities. He won his first cap in Dublin in 1975 when I withdrew, and established himself the following season when a broken leg kept me out of consideration. And it was Bill who took over the captaincy when a back injury threatened to end my career. And, after I had regained the captaincy, it was Bill again who took over from me in Dublin in 1979 when I had to drop out at the last minute with flu. He has not looked back since, and has taken England to the Far East and the Grand Slam, and then the British Lions to South Africa.

He has certainly come a long way since asking me for advice, further, perhaps, than you would have expected from a forward of his ability. But he has worked hard at his game, and given his play a rough edge that was not there naturally. His development came on by leaps and bounds when he joined the 1977 Lions as a replacement for Nigel Horton; that was probably the turning point of his career. His friendly and unassuming manner has won many friends for English and British rugby, as has his wholehearted response to any challenge which has been put his way. Bill's form had nothing to do with that disastrous day in Dublin. A mix-up near England's line transformed a winning position into a defeat.

Although at that point in the championship, the side was settling down and several players were beginning to fulfil their potential, the selectors decided to make crucial and rash changes. I came back for the next game, as did John Watkins and Martin Cooper, and Peter Wheeler came in for his debut after having been a reserve for the 1974 Lions. Out went Peter Dixon, Alan Old and John Pullin; three of England's top players in the seventies. It takes years to gain experience like they had; now it was discarded in an instant.

The demise of such experienced campaigners did little for the confidence of the side. Relationships between players and selectors were at a low ebb, as there was little consistency of thought or deed. Players were forced into safety-first tactics, spending their valuable time concentrating on eliminating mistakes; the whole style of the side was an inhibitive one. With Alan Old out, not only had we lost our fly-half but our goal-kicker and the leader of the backs. Three players for the price of one, but he was still not wanted by the selectors. Peter Rossborough took over the goal-kicking duties, but 16 points against France, including a try, was not enough to save England, or himself. More changes were made for the visit to Cardiff. It was a frustrating period for England's supporters, too.

One incident against the French symbolized our ineptness.

We were pressing near the French line and, although we were trailing, we had begun to get on top. Fran called for a tapped penalty, so that we could use one of those intricate moves which John had us practising for hours during our squad sessions. These elaborate exercises require precision running to make them go like clockwork; this was obviously easier in the leisurely atmosphere of the training field.

Fran's signal for the short penalty delighted the crowd, who cheered loudly in the hope that this might inspire us into something special – like a try! All these moves had a code, and I was normally involved in some way. Unfortunately, when Fran's call came back, my mind couldn't register the move with the signal. My philosophy has always been 'When in doubt, look busy', which I did. Sadly, I should not have been involved and I managed to get under everyone's feet. The move disintegrated into chaos. The groan from the crowd echoed around Twickenham and I just looked for a suitable hole to crawl into, especially when I took a look at Fran's face. We had the French under pressure, but my untimely intervention helped to restore their morale, and England tumbled to defeat.

The heads rolled again. As well as Peter Rossborough, who had never played more than two consecutive games for England, John Watkins was left out. So was Andy Ripley, after eighteen games on the trot. His omission meant my first outing for my country at number eight, with Nigel Horton coming in to partner Chris Ralston in the second row. Peter Dixon's return only showed that the selectors could not make up their minds. In fact Peter had to withdraw because of injury and John Watkins came back in, as did another player who had frequently been mucked around by the selectors – Tony Jorden.

But the side was going nowhere ... another heavy defeat followed. Jan Webster and Peter Wheeler had been injured during the game and were replaced by Steve Smith and John Pullin. Already we were guaranteed our third wooden spoon in four years, but we were going to have to beat the Scots to prevent them from winning their first Triple Crown since 1938 and to stop us registering our second-ever whitewash.

The axe was swung with ever greater ferocity this time and seven changes were made. No wonder the fans were left shaking their heads and wondering where it was all going to end. The most famous name missing was David Duckham, who was dropped for the first time in a thirty-three-cap career. His replacement was Alan Morley. We had a new combination at half-back; Neil Bennett came in for his first cap and Jacko Page came in from the cold for his first international since 1971. As for me, I was back to lock and Andy Ripley returned at number eight. Dave Rollitt was on the flank after a six-year absence from England's scrum, having been away from the scene longer than Jacko. Fran was injured; Mike Burton took his place at prop and Tony Neary assumed the captaincy. Talk about trial and error.

Yet we salvaged some pride with a 7 points to 6 victory, although the Scots missed two relatively simple penalty chances that would have brought them the Calcutta Cup and the Triple Crown. The only try came when Alan Morley won a controversial touch-down just ahead of Andy Irvine. This was not the sort of England side John Burgess had expected when he took over the role of coach. He worked us hard, probably too hard, but to little effect. Somehow, he could not work the same magic that had taken Lancashire to the top.

The situation only got worse. Relationships between players and selectors nearly reached breaking point with the announcement of the twenty-five-strong tour party that was to visit Australia that summer.

The seeds of another unsuccessful expedition were well and truly sown back in London. The selectors could not make up their minds whether to go for youth or experience; they had had enough choices – twenty-eight players had been used in the championship! Their own actions of the previous months only confused what was fast becoming a lottery and many of the names in this party could have been pulled out of a hat.

I still seemed to be in favour, but nobody was sure of anything in this atmosphere. The gravest errors were made in the choice of the fly-halves and scrum-halves. All the international experience this quartet had was a single appearance by Neil Bennett; Alan Wordsworth, Brian Ashton and Peter Kingston were all untried. Half-back is such a crucial area that you can't undertake any sort of tour without experience and control in this department.

We were to learn that lesson very quickly in Australia.

Our first sign of trouble was when we came across the Phantom Puncher. As the name suggests, he would deliver a quick blow with his fist and then disappear before any identification or retribution could be made. By a process of elimination, the finger of suspicion eventually found the vanishing culprit, one Steve Finnane, a prop who relished the publicity and spent the rest of his playing career living up to his notorious reputation.

Our record in the run-in to the first test at Sydney was pretty dismal. We suffered two defeats in those opening four matches, including a 13 points to 14 loss at the hands of the New South Wales Country fifteen. This was my first encounter with the famous up-your-jumper penalty move originated by John Hipwell's side. There is a famous photograph of this incident with yours truly looking over the top looking rather bemused. I was!

We were certainly not prepared for the first test. I partnered Neil Mantell in the second row; he was one of five new caps in the side, along with Peter Butler, Andy Maxwell, Barry Nelmes, who had been flown out, and Peter Kingston. Fran Cotton had been injured in the defeat by Sydney and was to take no further part.

The Sydney sports ground is a marvellous setting, but as the game progressed I began to wonder if referee Cooney was ever going to allow us to play rugby. His biased view of the action encouraged the home side to think it was pommie-bashing time. At almost every turn there were incidents ... and not your normal one-to-one arguments. Usually we were badly outnumbered; I remember on one occasion trying to slug it out with five of them. We lost Tony Neary with damaged ribs which ended his run of consecutive appearances since his debut in 1971. His departure lowered my morale considerably. Bill Beaumont came on, as did Alan Words-worth, for his only spell of international rugby, when Neil

Bennett had to leave the field.

Although the Wallabies deserved their victory and were the better side on the day, their tactics left me feeling cheated and concussed. The outcome was that I ended up in the toilet bawling my eyes out for about 20 minutes. The only other time that happened was in the first year of the national knock-out when Gosforth played Halifax. The tension and pressure of such a violent encounter had to be released somehow and tears were my way. Once it was over, I felt a lot better. God knows what it is like when the cricketers play there ... the tension must be almost unbearable. Rugby union is only a second-rate game in Australia, but it still attracts its devoted band of followers. That devotion is heightened by the fear that any failure might lead to their game disappearing under the dominance of the league code.

We were beginning to run out of players. The call was made to London for replacements. Brian Ashton had to return home because of domestic trouble and Ian Orum, another uncapped scrum-half, took his place. The injuries to Neil Bennett and Tony Neary ended their tours and at last some commonsense prevailed when Alan Old and Peter Dixon flew out to join the party. Alan played a valuable part in the second test, while Peter made the journey for eighty minutes of rugby against a Queensland Country fifteen. It was crazy that players of that calibre were not out there with us in the first place.

The second test was probably the most amazing game of rugby I have ever had the misfortune to play in. We had heard stories about the extreme attitude of their coach David Brockhoff to winning at any costs and the first test had given us experience of this at first hand. His fanaticism made John Burgess seem like a meek, easy-going liberal. At least John was always fair. Brockhoff was like a First World War general who sent his men into battle irrespective of the consequences. The ironic thing was that we were in no position to mount much of a real threat. Because of bad selection and crucial injuries, we did not have the experienced players to mount a serious attack.

It made little difference. At the kick-off the first assault wave hit us. We could not believe this was happening, but their commando unit continued their softening-up process at the next set-pieces. The scene was something like a bar-room brawl in a John Wayne movie; even watching this sorry spectacle on television afterwards, it was difficult to believe our eyes. The attacks were so premeditated that, if Bill Beaumont and Barry Nelmes had been set upon in the street like that, some of the Australian forwards would just now be coming up for parole.

. It came as no surprise when a player left the field in the first five minutes. The only trouble was that he was an Englishman. Mike Burton rounded off a memorable year by being dismissed for the second time and earning the title, first England player to be sent off in an international. In January, after being selected for the opening match against Ireland, he had been ordered off the field while playing for Gloucestershire against Hertfordshire in the county championship quarter-final. His sweeping bow to the committee box had brought widespread publicity and his dropping from the England team. His suspension was for four weeks, but his exile could have lasted a long time from the national team because Fran was captain and 'Stack' Stevens was in fine form. But Mickey returned to the side for the Calcutta Cup when Fran was injured.

His Gloucester upbringing would not allow the intimidation in Australia to go unpunished. For such an experienced operator, though, he threw caution to the wind by tackling their wing Doug Osborne late, very late, in the wide open spaces and in full view of everybody. Off he had to go, with referee Bob Burnett pointing the way, to the delight of the baying crowd whose sole philosophy of life was geared round the idea that: 'All poms are bastards.'

Down to fourteen men, our problems continued when Bill Beaumont had to go off for four stitches above his eye, the same number as I needed afterwards. We fought back and actually led by 15 points to 9 at half-time. Alan Old was keeping us ahead, a phenomenal display considering he had just flown across the world and virtually stepped off the plane onto the field.

One of Australia's front-line hit-men was flanker Ray Price, whose main task all afternoon was to hound and hit Alan Old at every opportunity, with or without the ball. One such late tackle won us a penalty. I will always treasure the look of amazement on the Aussies' faces as the dazed Alan Old picked himself up off the deck before rattling over the penalty from fully fifty yards. But the game was lost as they ran up 21 points in the second half, although I scored a consolation try near the end.

The test series may have been lost and over, but the aftermath of Mickey's sending-off was just beginning and some sensible soul had had the brainwave to organize a match against a Queensland Country fifteen to finish up with. Mickey received a severe caution; no doubt the television evidence showed just how provoked the England players were and this was taken into consideration. The Australians denied any planned assaults, but it was obvious to everybody that they had come onto the field so psyched up that any movement or gesture by us was seen as a physical threat to their authority. I said to David Brockhoff that if they had to resort to these tactics to win, then it hardly seemed worth playing. But it has always been an Australian characteristic to try continually to prove themselves whatever they do.

I think the person I disliked most on their side, even taking into account the Phantom Puncher, and Ray Price and Stuart MacDougal, was the hooker, Peter Norton. This man was a prime instigator of the trouble in the second test and seemed to have a real chip on his shoulder. Like a venomous snake spitting poison he hurled abuse at us as individuals and at our origins. Which was strange because he was English, too, and had left the mother country to teach in Australia. I don't think I would like my kids to come across his attitude or influence in the classroom. It was as though he felt he had betrayed his birthright and tried to hide his feelings of guilt by attacking England in any way he could.

Ray Price, his long blond hair flowing in the fray, was another who didn't know when to stop, although he was an immensely talented footballer. So were many of his colleagues in the Australian scrum, but they devoted their energies to other matters. Possibly they would have earned world-class

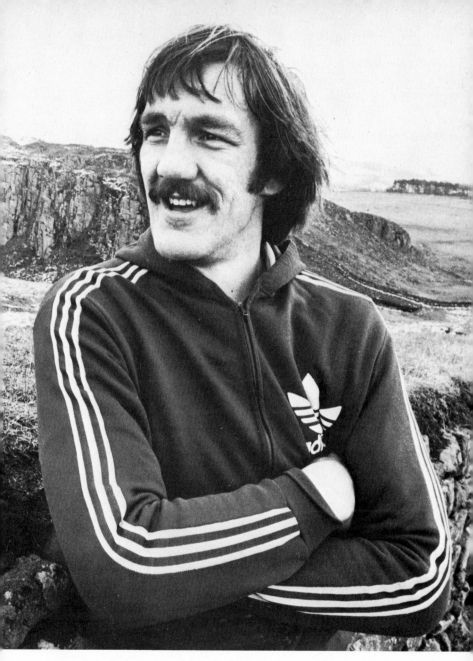

Surveying my territory as captain of England in 1977. Behind me is Hadrian's Wall, but I was waiting to repel the Scottish invaders at Twickenham, not here

On the way to manhood!

Above left: The proud recipient of the 1965 F.E. Harrison Trophy award to the outstanding schoolboy sportsman in Blackpool. With me is the top girl

Above right: Being so tall is an obvious asset in basketball as well as rugby

Below: The outdoor life was an important part of my youth. My companions on this particular hike are Bob Hopcroft and Jenny Martin

Me and my shadow: the two new caps for the 1973 game against Ireland — scrum-half Steve Smith and me

Opposite, above: It's always a good idea for a forward to get into the try-scoring act in the final trial, and Alan Old's tackle was not enough to stop me here in 1972

Opposite below: My first big game, against the 1969—70 South Africans. The line-up is (*back row, left to right*): Jake Young (referee), Murray, Richards, Parker, Wakefield, myself, McKenzie, Hartley, Littlechild, McGeechan, Dowson (reserve); (*front row*): Williams (reserve), Young, Sheard, Arneil, Carter (captain), Tennick, Keen, Old, Pickering (reserve)

An out-of-season fixture as Kris and I are married at St Gabriel's Church in Heaton on 27 July 1971

My favourite team photograph. Syd Millar has just put us through a hard session at Stellenbosch and we are more than ready for the 1974 Springboks. The fifteen Lions are (*back row*): Phil Bennett, Fergus Slattery, J.P.R. Williams, Willie John, yours truly, Mervyn Davies, Fran Cotton; (*front row*): Gordon Brown, Bobby Windsor, Ian McLauchlan, Gareth Edwards, Ian McGeechan, Billy Steele, Dick Milliken and J.J. Williams

Andy Ripley is about the only one who would put up with my company as I try to learn to play the recorder in South Africa

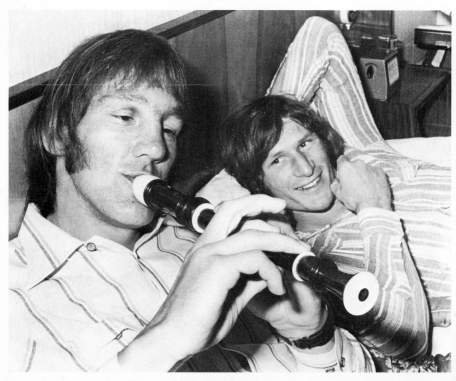

The try that never was: Chris Pope obviously wins the touch-down near the start of the fourth
test, but the try was given to me. I didn't complain

I was never fitter than in that Lions tour in 1974. I felt ready to take anyone on — as can be
seen here

The disgraceful outbreak of violence at the beginning of the second test in Australia in 1975. In the front of the picture Bill Beaumont is being given a terrible going-over by Peter Horton (2) and Ray Price (7)

The famous 'up your jumper' penalty move. No wonder I look rather bemused

reputations of a different kind had Brockhoff not been calling the shots. Watching the events on television in the clubhouse afterwards, I saw Ray Price make one of his blatantly illegal interventions. 'What a thug,' I shouted, knowing that Ray was only a few feet away. 'Soft Poms,' was his response, and we half grinned at each other. That such a conversation could be carried on at all, let alone in a good-humoured manner, would amaze a lot of people after what we had been through. But this social communication, even after the most bitter of contests, has always been rugby's safety valve.

Nothwithstanding this, the atmosphere after the second test was highly charged, not least because Australia were scheduled to make a tour of the UK in the autumn. John Burgess found it difficult to be polite to any Australian for the rest of the tour. The spectacle of the second test had not only been witnessed by manager Alec Lewis, but past-president of the RFU Ken Chapman and Tarn Bainbridge. There was even talk of abandoning England's section of the autumn visit. I was beginning to understand the fury and feeling that must have been generated by the famous cricket 'body-line' series in the early thirties.

Ken Chapman said at the time, 'I have been appalled at some of the matches I have seen on this tour, but my criticism is not confined to Australia. The Lions' method of using code 99 for mass retaliation did not help.' Actually, we were not experienced or organized enough to make that sort of reply; the trouble might not have got out of control if we had been. That is the reason Mickey took matters into his own hands.

The Australian president Bill McLaughlin came out with a more ambiguous statement. 'This violence must be left behind when we go on tour to Britain.' I had to agree. I was shocked that anybody wanted to play rugby that way. The fact that similar treatment was dished out to the Welsh a few years later was an indication of the wrong approach they had to the game out there. It is to be hoped that it will be the running talents of the Australia backs that will be remembered after the 1981–82 tour of Britain.

The violence overshadowed the fact that we had helped to bring about our failure, in terms of results. There is no substitute for experience and, if you are going to blood new players, then you have to introduce them into a winning environment if you hope to produce quality players. The fact that England did produce some quality players during the seventies was more a tribute to their individual tenacity and perseverence than to any pattern or philosophy adopted by the RFU or their various selection committees.

My own feelings on the tour were recorded in a letter I wrote to Kris after the first test. 'We play Queensland this afternoon and I am going to play on the flank with Rippers and David Rollitt. I feel bruised and battle-weary at present and I cannot say that I am enjoying the rugby. The test match on Saturday was a gruelling affair. They were very physical and I came off feeling as though I'd just been through fifteen rounds with Ali. It was quite a humiliating experience. We just haven't got enough strength in depth; however there is nothing to be done now.'

But the tour was not all bad and there were many happy memories off the field. In Sydney we came across an old friend in John 'Cruncher' Gray, a member of England's winning seven at Murrayfield in 1973. He had turned to rugby league and was now based in Australia, where he was a big star. John was a superb athlete and the superstar treatment and lifestyle suited him right down to the ground. We couldn't help feeling envious of his success, although it hadn't seemed to affect him as, with us, he was still the same old John.

After the second test, we spent a marvellous day on Compass Island, well away from all the controversy. After a splendid barbecue, our boat trip was reminiscent of such an occasion in South Africa. Back at the hotel, I had had enough and went to bed. I awoke suddenly with the realization that there was somebody in my room. It was Mickey Burton, desperately searching for something. When it dawned on me that he thought the wardrobe was the toilet, I leapt out of bed and pointed him in the right direction. It had been that sort of a tour.

6

England Whitewashed

Nobody now was in any doubt that England's international reputation was in tatters. Selectors were going through players like confetti; the more they experimented, the more problems they created.

The first shock of the new season was the resignation of John Burgess as coach. Australia had left him shattered. After such high hopes for England, his dreams were in the same state as the country's reputation. Now it was the turn of Bristol's Peter Colston to make an impression.

I pushed England's problems to the back of my mind as the new season began. After two years under David Robinson's leadership, I had been made captain of Gosforth. The club were now playing a much higher standard of rugby than when I had first joined.

Even the training was much more sophisticated now that Jack Rowell had taken over as coach. Jack was a marvellous influence, not so much by virtue of what he knew as a tactician, but because of what he knew about us. In reality, people like David Robinson, Peter Dixon and myself ran the sessions, but Jack was the ringmaster, making sure the whole show ran smoothly. He would consult Peter, cajole Robbo, tell Malcolm to shut up – which he seldom did – and always referred to me as the deckchair attendant.

The squad of players at Gosforth were now about the best in the country. The front row, made up of Colin White, Duncan Madsen and Andy Cutter, was like a rock, seldom in trouble. With Terry Roberts and either Jack Hedley or John Short making up the engine-room, us prima donnas in the back row could really enjoy ourselves, for the scrummage was so secure there was seldom a need to stay down.

There was no shortage of skill behind the scrum. In the number nine shirt was one of the most consistent scrum-halves in the country, who could also kick goals from any-where – and frequently did. Malcolm Young was a prime example of England not using the talent available. Richard Breakey was at fly-half; although rather unpredictable, his hands were excellent and he has since confirmed his potential. One of the centres was Ken Britten, who like Colin White had defected from Northern. Ken was an elusive talent, but suffered from a chronic shoulder condition which eventually led to his early retirement from the game. His partner was Harry Patrick, a great club servant and Geordie comedian whose greatest asset, as far as I was concerned, was providing Peter and I with after-match cigarettes. Outside him on the wing was Steve Gustard, who was and still is working at being a legend in his own lifetime. His abrasive and uncompromis-ing running was very similar to that of the man on the other wing, David Carr. David in full flight was a fearful sight and sometimes his physical aggression could lead him into trouble. The previous season he had been sent off in our John Player Cup quarter-final match against Bedford; he never really recovered from that incident. Brian Patrick was still directing operations at full-back. These were the men who transformed a little-known northern club into a position of national prominence.

Several members of Gosforth, including yours truly, were selected for the North East Counties game against the visiting Australians. How would they behave away from the safety of home? Dave Brockhoff was still in charge and Finnane, Price and Horton were among the tourists. Wisely, they abandoned their fist-flying approach. In a thrilling match, we went down by the odd point in 43. Considering we had only been through a couple of training sessions, it proved again that there were England-calibre players around – they just needed pointing in the right direction.

The England selection system was changed yet again, so that the national side played the regions before the final trial. I played at number eight for England. We went down to an embarrassing 10 points to 18 defeat against the North and Midlands. Just the confidence-boosting start we did not need!

The following Saturday the opposition was the South and South West. Colin White and Peter Dixon were both on the bench for the Sunday session, and so joined me on the journey down. Colin and I picked up a two-litre Cortina at Newcastle airport, gathered Peter at Durham and headed for Cheltenham, where we were to spend the night. A bad accident on the M6 meant a slow start, so I sprawled out in the back with Peter and Colin sharing the driving. I realized the folly of my action when we stopped just outside Cheltenham for petrol. As I stretched over to open the boot to get some money out, there was a sudden pain in my back as though someone had plunged a blade in my back.

Not again! For the third time in three years, I'd been caught out like this. This first time had been in 1974 at North Berwick as I bent down to pick up a ball. The second occasion was just before the England game in 1975 against Ireland. During lunch, the waiter had brought me apple pie and ice cream when suddenly I was incapacitated again. Now the scene was a service station. I broke out in a cold sweat. It is very difficult not to panic as the feeling of paralysis stays with you. In order to make it go, you have to relax, but an instinctive tenseness makes it impossible.

Peter and Colin helped me back into the car and, at our destination, into the hotel. Not for the first time, I had to go and face Alec Lewis, the chairman of selectors. Such approaches were becoming regular; he must have been getting sick of seeing one of England's supposedly top physical specimens repeatedly breaking down in the unlikeliest places.

I slouched off to bed with a few painkilling tablets, but even a good night's sleep did not ease the pain. I missed the final trial and the international against the Australians. England introduced Mike Lampkowski, Barrie Corless and Mark Keyworth for that match, although there was no place for David Rollitt who had had such a marvellous tour of Australia only a few months before. David Duckham did return, though, and scored one of the three tries in the 23 points to 6 victory. Once again, the talk was of another England revival;

it should have been obvious to anyone with a modicum of sense that the ever-widening cracks had merely been covered with thicker paper than usual.

A week later I had made my come-back game, leading Gosforth against Glasgow Academicals. The following Saturday was the England versus Wales match. I travelled to London with Gosforth for a game against Richmond in the morning. One or two of the England lads, including David Duckham and Andy Ripley, had come along to watch, as well as a couple of the selectors. Despite the vigorous contest, my back felt good and I was moving around with no problems at all. I would show the selectors that they need have no worries about my fitness after this performance. But my season came dramatically to a halt during the second half. For once, the blame couldn't be put on my back; with my leg trapped in a maul, someone hit me from out of the blue and I spun round violently. Unfortunately, my leg was unable to perform the same action and there was a loud crack as I hurtled towards the ground. My immediate thought was that the leg was broken, but I was able to hobble off with the assistance of Jack Rowell. While lying on the ground, I heard John Hedley threaten, 'Ey up; we're not going to let them get away with that.'

They did not and proceeded to annihilate Richmond, who had a man sent off. It was a very physical game, with several ugly incidents, but I did not attribute my injury to dirty play. Sadly, my fears were confirmed when I went to Roehampton Hospital, where X-rays revealed I had a broken leg; a spiral fracture of the lower left fibula, to be exact. All the way to London just for that!

The leg was put in plaster and doctors thought that I would be out of action for at least six months. So, that was the end of my international challenge for that season, the only consolation being that the newspapers could not blame my back this time.

The next weeks were a real drag. After being very active, there is nothing more frustrating than to find that even the simplest chores are a major exercise. But at least I was around to help Kris in the final stages of her pregnancy, although

I nearly missed the actual birth. I had committed myself to speak at a dinner in Leeds, but just before I rose to my feet I received a note to say Kris had been taken into hospital – I said my few words and rushed to Newcastle General Hospital, just in time to watch the arrival of Simon James Uttley – a great moment.

My inactivity was not helped by watching the shambling performances of the England team as they headed with such determination for the bottom of the championship yet again. On the afternoon after I had broken my leg, two tries by JPR and one by Gareth – both familiar thorns in the sides of English flesh – had brought Wales to victory. Scotland was the next stop, but England's half-time lead of 12 points to 9 was overhauled as Scotland surged ahead. Things couldn't get worse; they did.

A half-time lead, this time 9–nil against the Irish was surely the start of a recovery. Wrong again. Ireland returned home with a 13 points to 12 win. The only hope of salvation that remained was the daunting prospect of a trip to Paris to meet a French side that had narrowly failed to prevent Wales from winning the Grand Slam.

If any game symbolized the depth to which English rugby had sunk, this was it. Martin Cooper was selected at fly-half although he had been injured and had not played for a couple of weeks. Then the selectors, having taken a risk that they did not know existed, failed him in a fitness test in Paris. Logically, in a normal society, I would have expected the replacement, Alan Old, automatically to come into the side; you could not ask for a better back-up man. Instead, for some inexplicable reason they sent for Gloucester's Chris Williams so that he could make his only England appearance. Alan took the news badly and who could blame him? . . . it was an unbelievable turn-about. Peter Wheeler also withdrew through injury at the eleventh hour and John Pullin returned for his forty-second and final game for England. What a tragic end to such a magnificent career.

Every mistake – playing and selectorial – was on show that day. France ran in six tries and ran up 30 points. Still, England were let off lightly – the French, but for poor finishing and lack of concentration, could have scored 60. England's rugby was at the bottom of the pile and in a sorry state. Their list of honours was mounting – four wooden spoons in five years and now their second-ever whitewash.

This is probably a good opportunity to assess what the problems were and how they had arisen. Many of us who struggled through the seventies were still there in the Grand Slam year of 1980, so I can only look back on the standard of selection in this period as being the principal reason for our failure. During these two years, 1975 and 1976, England managed to lose nine of the eleven internationals they took part in; the body-count for those two years was an amazing forty-six players. And you have to add to that total, the five uncapped players on the Australian visit. Statistics which even today make me shudder.

The strongest influence in the game at this time was the north, where Lancashire were first to emerge under John Burgess and then another great innovator Dick Greenwood. Their strength of will and professional approach to the game made everybody sit up and take notice. Danie Serfontein and John Elders then helped to produce a similar reaction in Northumberland and the north was geared up to dominate English rugby for the next decade.

On the club scene, the projection of Gosforth to prominence in the north east and of initially Broughton Park and latterly Liverpool and Sale in the north west provided a solid base of real talent and expertise. The switch in power coincided with the decline of the great Midlands clubs like Coventry and Northampton, as well as the country's general dissatisfaction with the game down in the south east. All these factors combined to give the selectors an ideal opportunity to rebuild after a number of devastating defeats.

The selectors, though, did not recognize that the strength of the regional sides of the north and the south west was in their strong area identification, particularly with men like John Burgess and Des Seabrook at the helm. For me, some of those regional matches for the North were among the happiest and most satisfying of my career. Rather than to capitalize on the

88

advantage of good morale, the actions of those picking the national side seemed designed to destroy any spirit that had been built up.

Nothing was more typical of the selectors' inadequacies than their attitude to the half-back problem. Their actions were of complete wonderment to me. Rather than pick tried and experienced partnerships which were available – like that of Malcolm Young and Alan Old or of Jan Webster and John Finlan – they decided on a more complicated solution. They continued their lemming-like experiments, always with the bizarre idea that something magical might happen between a fly-half and unfamiliar scrum-half in the middle of an England international. And, surprise, surprise, when nothing did happen and another game was lost, it was back to the drawing board and abstruse formulae in their search for the perfect couple.

While the selectors were picking the teams with all the abandonment of an Arab oil sheikh at the roulette wheel, risk was a characteristic that was visibly vanishing from the play of those bidding for a place in the national side. Everybody's first concern at the time was to get through eighty minutes of rugby without taking a chance or making a mistake. They saw this attitude, quite rightly at the time, as their best hope of reaching the big time and providing the selectors with the type of player they wanted. True, that might have been the best way to further your career, but it was hardly likely to produce the sort of rugby that was going to win success for England in the competitive arena.

Yet, despite all this chopping and changing, England had a pack of forwards who were capable of beating the best in the world. Usually, though, after dominating the field for an hour, we would look up at the scoreboard to see that all this pressure had hardly been turned into points, if at all.

Then, when we saw the opposition making the most, or at least better, use of their limited opportunities and possession, our heads would not surprisingly drop as we became despondent and almost neurotic. It was not going to be our day, yet again. That was the same old story throughout the seventies.

It was not only among the forwards that we had players

capable of winning matches. Despite rumours to the contrary, England did have talented, skilful, running three-quarters. What those in charge never seemed to realize is that selecting is not just about picking the best fifteen players available; it is about arriving at the best combination of players. Often their weak choices in crucial areas would affect the whole potential of the team.

Alastair Hignell was a classic case in point. One of the most talented sportsmen I have ever come across, he could play full-back or scrum-half. The scrum-half spot was where he had shone for England Schools, while full-back was his place at Cambridge University and where he won his England shirt, in Australia in 1975. Unfortunately, Alastair was frequently troubled by ankle trouble, which needed rest to clear up. Even more unfortunately, the selectors felt they could not do without him. Several times the Flying Pig – as he was affectionately known – played for his country while not fully fit, although he never let England down. Consequently, the supporters never had a chance to see him at his very best in an England jersey, basically because he was either still restricted by injury or, having recovered, had not been allowed the time to train sufficiently to get his ample frame in shape.

One difference between these days and 1980, the year of the Grand Slam – which seemed the impossible dream in the seventies – was that everybody in the 1980 team was there on merit. It was also the side the players wanted. You always knew that there was someone behind you, backing you up all the way, on and off the field. That was the complete team effort, with regional pride being used to benefit England; everybody's energy was directed towards helping the side to achieve success. Even in 1976, though, I was convinced that we had the players available; it all seemed to boil down to getting it right on the night – which was England's other great problem. The system in England was just not geared to a competitive atmosphere and, when players had to react under pressure in internationals, they were liable to make mistakes in critical positions that cost us dear.

At least Gosforth were getting it right as they strove to the final of the John Player Cup for the first time. Malcolm Young took over the captaincy while I was incapacitated, and I hobbled around giving everyone a hard time under the pretext of helping Jack Rowell with the coaching. Hartlepool Rovers, Liverpool, Roundhay and Sale were our victims on the way to Twickenham.

Our battle with Sale in the semi-final was to determine which northern team would be the first to reach the final in the five years of competition. It was a rugged game with Fran Cotton leaving the field nine minutes before the end at the referee's request after an incident with Malcolm Young. Our opponents in the final were Rosslyn Park, who had been beaten at the last stage the previous year by Bedford. They were out of luck again. Their chances suffered a severe blow when Bob Mordell was sent off in the opening minutes by referee Norman Sanson. I had some sympathy for Bob, who had just reacted too violently to some jersey-pulling from a wily old Gosforth campaigner. The London side put up a brave struggle and it was only in the final quarter that we made the game safe. Rosslyn Park had in fact led by 14 points to 7 before tries from Terry Roberts, Steve Gustard (his forty-second of that season) and David Robinson, plus two conversions, gave Gosforth a 23 points to 14 victory. My lasting memory of that day concerns those two great characters, Steve Gustard and Harry Patrick. Both were lazing after the match in the same individual Twickenham bath. Not only were they still kitted out, but Steve was clutching a bottle of champagne while Harry was smoking a large cigar à la Clint Eastwood. And the pair were grinning from ear to ear.

7

Captain of England
... To Be Continued

During the summer, I was re-elected captain of Gosforth for a second term; maybe the club hoped that I might put in a full term of office this time! Although the leg was out of plaster, it did not feel right so I was out training early in July. At the time there was some very premature talk that I might be a likely candidate for the England captaincy, but I did not really take much notice. My immediate ambitions were just to get fit and regain my place in the side.

Gosforth's first big outing of the season was a trip across the border to play West of Scotland. The 'Rugby Special' cameras were in attendance and it looked the ideal opportunity to press my claims early. Our new coach was Mike Mahoney – Jack Rowell had taken up an appointment in Bath – but our form that day hardly impressed him, or anyone else for that matter. The match was a typical start-of-the-season encounter, with too much energy wasted and too many mistakes. Watching our efforts on the 'box' afterwards was agonizing; all the action seemed to be taking place at a pedestrian pace.

For other reasons that Scottish trip still lives in my memory. There is a very posh and plush upstairs bar at Burnbrae where the clientele and accents would do Miss (or should it now be Ms?) Jean Brodie proud. That evening, the cocktail party scene was rudely interrupted by Harry Patrick and David Robinson making an entrance reminiscent of the Wild West. The American connection continued as the final member of this rough-looking trio ambled in – a donkey who had been lazing around in a neighbouring field. Perhaps after watching our exploits that afternoon, he fancied his chances of getting into the Gosforth side! Still, his presence livened up the proceedings, but I was not altogether certain he was keeping the right sort of company.

Not surprisingly, England's selection panel had been changed yet again. Sandy Sanders was back as chairman in place of Alec Lewis. I always got on well with Sandy, as he managed to bridge that gap between players and the alikadoos. Whilst never regarded as one of the boys, he was honest, straight and as keen for success as the players. Even with him back at the head of the magnificent seven, though, the build-up to the championship was as chaotic as ever, giving no indication that anything had changed.

It had not as far as I was concerned. Injuries were again the order of the day. First I popped a rib cartilage, and then a badly bruised shoulder kept me out of the Probables–Possibles trial match in the middle of December. It was just as well, too, because the senior side were toppled to the tune of 6–nil. Those points came from the boot of Alastair Hignell, who was the subject of an atrocious scrum-half experiment that afternoon. The selectors quickly realized the folly of their actions and Alastair was returned to full-back for the England team that was to face The Rest on New Year's Day. What the selectors could have been trying to do in the first place is beyond me.

More importantly for me, the announcement of that New Year's Day side meant I was only one game away from the ultimate honour of leading my country on to the international field. The England side I captained contained only two of the Probable's pack from that first game. Out went the back row comprising Steve Callum, Garry Adey and Andy Ripley; they were replaced by Mike Rafter, myself and Peter Dixon.

One name very conspicuous by its absence was that of Tony Neary. True, his seven games as England's captain only brought two victories and it was always on the cards that he might lose the captaincy. But nobody expected that he would be denied the right of a trial in which to stake his claims for a spot on the flank. The selectors made it obvious that they didn't want him around and that they were not going to risk the chance of being shown up by him in the trial. Such neglect was scandalous, but Tony lost neither faith nor form and returned to have the last laugh as England's most capped player of all time.

Although my own appearances had been limited I looked forward to the Barbarians' game against Leicester at the end of December to give me some much-needed match practice. And I got it – all three minutes of it – before being carried off badly concussed. What worried me more was a bout of vomiting an hour after the game: the trial was only a few days away. A consultation with a specialist put my mind at rest.

Despite one or two withdrawals, the trial for once went according to plan and form with England winning by 20 points to 3. The selectors made one change to that winning team for the opening game – Bill Beaumont came in, replacing Llanelli's Roger Powell. This 'as you were' meant I became England's seventeenth captain since Richard Sharp had led them to the 1963 championship. That fact alone emphasized that my head was on the chopping block; four captains had lasted one match apiece, three more had managed a couple of games in charge and two had reached the grand total of three-time leaders. Not exactly the securest job around ... I think someone once compared it to being president of a South American republic. Since that last championship success, England had the appalling record of eighteen wins in sixty-eight games and had averaged one win per season for the past eight years.

But the past was not my concern. The announcement of the team was a day of celebration for Gosforth. Not only was I number eight and captain, but Peter Dixon was a back-row colleague. The whole club was overjoyed also to see that Malcolm Young, now thirty-one and seven years older than when he had acted as a replacement, was to win a full cap at last. When you consider some of the scrum-halves who had been chosen in front of him during the seventies, it is a wonder he did not give up in disgust. The England roll of honour for scrum-half was as bad as that for the captaincy – seventeen had occupied the position since Dickie Jeeps's retirement in 1962. By a quirk of fate, Dickie was the president of the RFU this year and he rather cruelly pointed out that he was younger when he gave up after twenty-four international appearances and three Lions tours than Malcolm was now.

Sandy had already stated his selection policy. 'I see nothing wrong in choosing a side that we hope will make it difficult for opponents to score.' Not exactly a blueprint for attacking rugby, but a sensible approach when you consider that England let in thirteen tries in 1976. While hoping to eliminate mistakes, I thought the back line had plenty of potential which they should try to show off in the Calcutta Cup.

I was delighted to be captain ... I have even kept a cutting with the traditional 'over the moon' comment. I had thought the selectors might have tried Fran Cotton or Peter Dixon again, or maybe Peter Wheeler who had led the Probables side in the trial. Yet the call was for change, and not being personally involved in the disasters of 1976 might have counted in my favour.

Trying to read the minds of selectors is an impossible task, but I think that my honest, no-nonsense approach appealed to them as much as anything else. I looked on the honour as a natural progression after captaining club and county, and England seemed to favour forwards for their leaders. You have to go all the way back to Bob Hiller in 1972 to find the last person outside the scrum to have captained England. Since then Peter Dixon, John Pullin, Fran Cotton, Tony Neary, myself and Bill Beaumont have all been given the job. It is incredible to realize that all of us, except John Pullin, were to play on that memorable day of the North's triumph over the All Blacks at Otley in 1979. Surely, few packs can have had such experience as that.

To me the captaincy was all a matter of self-confidence. Off the field, occasionally, I would feel self-doubts creeping in, but it only took a few steps back onto the pitch to recover my belief in my own ability. Others seemed to respect my opinions and integrity. As in school, others were aware of my leadership qualities probably before I was.

I was well aware that the opening game would set the tone for the rest of the season. The fact that Scotland were the opponents was to our advantage. Despite a shortage of world-class players, the Scottish selectors had made the mistake of dropping their captain Ian McLauchlan – a move that bordered on suicide. If there was one thing this fierce warrior liked better than playing the English, it was beating them. Also absent was Gordon Brown, who was under a sixteen week suspension after being sent off for fighting during an inter-district match at Murrayfield. Ian McGeechan took over the captaincy and their front row included the fourth member of the Gosforth club to play in this match, Duncan Madsen.

If there was an obvious weakness in the Scotland team, it was to be found in the back row, comprising Alex Brewster, Donald MacDonald (both winning their first caps) and Wilson Lauder; that was an area we would try to expose and exploit. The Scots are notoriously bad travellers and to make my leadership debut at Twickenham would take much of the pressure off.

Everyone was aware that we were starting from scratch. Only four remained from that drubbing in Paris. There were three new caps as well as Malcolm Young – Robin Cowling, Mike Rafter and Charles Kent. My appointment as captain also marked a notable hat-trick for Gosforth. Both Arthur Smith (Scotland) and Ray McLoughlin (Ireland) had captained their countries while serving as skippers at the club. Quite an achievement.

After the relative peace and quiet of the previous season, I was now courted from all directions for my opinions about who was going to take the title. International rugby is so unpredictable that looking ahead can be a very hazardous occupation. Here are my thoughts from the *Sunday Times* before the 1977 campaign.

We are a workmanlike side, and initially we probably won't do great things. Our main tactic is to make as few mistakes as possible. Because of injuries, I've been out of international rugby for a whole season, so at the moment what I want to do is to last a full eighty minutes. Playing Wales down in Cardiff is a challenge, but you must keep a sense of proportion when playing there. You are aware of the vast noise and if you are going badly it doesn't help to have that crowd on your back baying. They can do things from the oddest of places on the field; they can absorb limitless punishment and pressure, and then hit back and they have excellent players in key positions. Plus they have the Welsh arrogance. But it will be interesting to see how they do without Mervyn Davies. Against Ireland it won't be quite the same as it was four years ago, when we were so overwhelmed by their warm welcome for even going there that we lost. That was my first cap. Against Scotland I'm glad we don't have to travel to our bogey ground. For us it is a great advantage to have our first game at Twickenham because we must fancy our chances at home. This season we must take the chances that are offered to us; the Welsh do and that is why they have done so well. Against them last season we wasted two chances early on. Then suddenly against the run of play Gareth Edwards grabbed that try. When that happened you could see the England boys saying to themselves, 'we're struggling'. And they were from that point on. Wales must be favourites for this year's Triple Crown, and the other three countries are all level. I don't bet, but I'm confident that we can do better than finishing last.

So were the rest of the players; everyone seemed keen to purge themselves of the previous season's efforts and applied themselves accordingly. For once the build-up went smoothly and the mood was excellent on the Friday night gathering. We would soon see if the selectors had made the right choice as captain, I thought as I got to my feet for my team talk. I had based it, I hoped, on common sense and the things we had to come to terms with. I have kept the rough notes on which my talk was based.

Rugby is a simple game. We must ensure that as few mistakes are made as possible, both as individuals and as a unit. Mistakes are what have let English rugby down in the seventies. We can only win if we get into their half of the field and we must try and stay as close to their line for as long as possible. As a general rule, we will only expand our game as we move upfield. Nothing must be static. Man for man we are better than the Scots, and we are a better team, too; so we are going to win. You've all been picked because of particular strengths, so play as you would normally do for your club. You can be safe in the knowledge that the other fourteen players are as good as, if not better than yourself.

We must pressure the Scots into mistakes and capitalize on these opportunities. Tie up the ball immediately – none of this hot-potato stuff. If we fall behind, keep your heads up and keep battling away.

If there's any rough stuff, then step in to help a team-mate; no stand-up bouts, use your imagination. Concentration must be of the highest order – following up kicks, keeping on the pressure; get on top of your opposite number and try and psyche him out. Our penalties will either go to Nigel or Frannie; on theirs, get into position quickly and pick out your man; go up in a line together. This is a game about percentages. The fewer mistakes, the greater the chance of winning. Remember, we must communicate; if you're not sure, ask. Coops, make sure everybody in the back knows what's going on. Up front, the back-row moves can only be carried out when we are going forward with good channel ball. Remember, don't throw the ball away in the tackle, make it available; go forward as a unit.

It may all sound a bit obvious, even corny, but the simple things needed saying at this point. When I had finished speaking, one or two looked as if they were ready to take the field there and then; I hoped they would not have gone off the boil by tomorrow.

Everyone was in a confident mood as we took the field. Reading the many congratulatory telegrams had helped to ease my own pre-match nerves. One from Tony Neary showed his unselfish concern for England, even though for the first time since 1971 he was not involved personally.

Scotland took an early 3–nil lead, but the English heads didn't drop as we showed the determination and courage that the Twickenham crowd had been waiting a decade for. That was the commitment and loyalty for which John Burgess had been searching. We proceeded to run in four tries, twice as many as in the whole of the previous season. Scotland managed some sort of parity in the line-out, but we ruled everywhere else. The Twickenham crowd roared to see such sport ... I have never heard that noise bettered in any other rugby stadium in the world.

My day was made complete when I dived over for the final try after picking the ball up from a scrum. Although I was trapped under a pile of bodies, I did manage to wave one of my legs in the air as a signal to mark unequivocally the start of England's revival (one or two of the Gosforth players wanted to know how much Adidas had paid me for that free bit of advertising on prime television time). As fate would have it, I was not on the field when the final whistle went. My nose had come into collision with Martin Cooper's head and something had to give. The contact went with form and my nose was spread even further across my face. Leaving before that final whistle was a great disappointment because I desperately wanted to share that moment with the lads who had come up with the goods for me and England. Doctor Leo was again my escort – I'm surprised there wasn't talk – and he proceeded to shove what seemed like yards of vaseline tape up my nose – which caused some embarrassing moments during the evening.

Nothing, though, could dampen the euphoria that day. English rugby was on its way back. Sandy was as delighted as we were to celebrate our first win in the championship for two years. Not only that, but the 26 points to 6 margin was the highest ever in the Calcutta Cup and England's biggest score in the Five Nations competition for a decade.

It could have been more, too, if Alastair Hignell had not missed five penalty and two conversion attempts.

Back in the dressing room all the talk was of winning, what we had achieved, nothing negative. Of course, the champagne flowed. Well, I say 'of course', but you learn over the years to take nothing for granted. Typically, one or two small examples of meanness and thoughtlessness spoilt the party, as the alikadoos came to the fore and the players were supposed to merge into the background again. Mickey Weston, always a players' man and considerate of our needs, had been the one to think of laying on the champagne. Such spoiling was frowned upon by some of the senior members of the committee. Mickey, to his credit, settled the bill himself rather than let squabbling overshadow what was surely a historic day for English rugby.

On the coach during the ride back to the Hilton, I inquired whether arrangements had been made for drinks in the captain's room so that the ladies could join us before the dinner. I was informed that the president had invited the players and selectors to his room for pre-dinner drinks. As usual, no mention was made of our wives and girlfriends; the system was not geared to catering for them and some of the older committee seemed surprised that we bothered to bring them along at all. Luckily, Sandy appreciated that the wives played a part, so permission was given for them to accompany us.

Players today give so much in terms of time and effort when they play for their countries that it is incomprehensible that even the basic details of making their lives a little easier are often not thought of. Wives also suffer: not only from their husbands' prolonged absences through training and travelling, but also from the pre-match tense build-up and the possible post-match depression.

Many of the old-timers, though, still regard the female of the species as a necessary evil. In some ways, the celebration of the game seemed to be too much trouble. Rugby is about thirty blokes running around a park on a Saturday afternoon, whether good, bad or indifferent. Yet, those thirty are the tip of the iceberg and they would like the back-up people to be involved. Still, all rugby authorities tend to disregard them or accept them grudgingly as a painful necessity. With a little forethought, life could run so smoothly.

As it is, a wife can have a hard time following her man around on his rugby adventures. When we lived in Newcastle, Kris would have to get up at 6 a.m. on Saturday to catch the train and arrive in London at midday. Her trek continued as the tube took her across London to Richmond. From there, she would normally have to walk to Twickenham, which is a fair old way, especially as she was carrying a case. She was able to leave that in the RFU office before taking her seat just in time for a 3 p.m. kick-off; by this point, she had been on the go for nine hours. After the match, we might be able to link up for a quick cup of tea before heading up town. The ladies' evening is a lot more organized now and they have their own dinner while the men go off to eat. It was not always so civilised, but times are changing ... slowly!

When you look at the perks the committee have (the option to buy twenty tickets for home games and one free trip away, accompanied, a year), then those of the players (two free tickets and the chance to buy four more) are treated shabbily. Don't get me wrong; I don't begrudge the committee their rewards – they work hard as unpaid servants of the game, putting in large amounts of time and effort. But it would be nice if the players were given the impression of feeling important for more than just eighty minutes four or five afternoons a season. International rugby players are adults and are expected to behave as such – it is a shame that they are treated like kids.

On a night such as this, what a shame that we were wasting time and energy on matters other than celebration. With everything going right for us on the field, then you would expect arrangements to run like clockwork off it.

Yet even with all this irritation, nothing could obliterate the mood of excitement our thundering victory had produced in us. We were all aware that Scotland were not the greatest side in the world, but after being so starved of success any crumb of comfort was gobbled up with glee. The players were more cautious than the press, who were overflowing in their praise of our performance and even of England's new leader. Obviously, I was glad we had started off with a win and pleased with the way the players had responded to my leadership, but there was still a long way to go. Dublin, our next destination, would be a real test.

The selectors were delighted and went as far as naming the same squad for the Irish match; the last time England had managed that was four years earlier. Ireland worried me far more than Scotland had. For a start they had won five games in a row against England and, also, that shrewd rugby brain Mike Gibson was back at fly-half, for his sixtieth international.

Our preparations were disrupted when Mike Rafter withdrew because of injury, but in Tony Neary we had an ideal replacement who had the respect of all the players. Somehow this confidence was not conveyed by the selectors in their dealings with the press. Sandy described the loss as a 'body blow', while Peter Colston added, 'We will miss Mike because having chosen him in the first place, we obviously wanted him. Tony, though, will give us another ball-winner in the line-out, but winning the ball on the ground is equally important.'

The selectors did have a thing at the time about flankers spending the afternoons on their backsides. Mike, Rafter the Grafter, was exactly what they wanted. But Tony will do for me any day.

He was magnificent that day in the mud of Lansdowne Road. The cold, drizzling weather guaranteed a gruelling forward battle and I had a tough time trying to cope with the considerable line-out talents of Willie Duggan. As it was, very little separated the sides and the game was eventually decided on the hour by some Moseley improvization. Nigel Horton, showing some adept footballing skill, kicked through and Martin Cooper was on hand to slither on the ball for the only score of the afternoon.

The actual rugby may not have remained in my memory, but that day in Ireland is special because it was the only time I ever played in the England back row with Peter Dixon and Tony Neary. To me, and to countless others, this was a great pity. Not only did our styles complement each other but we knew each other's game so well – the weaknesses as well as strengths. Those rare days when we did combine, like that of the North's 1979 win at Otley, only emphasized the mistake of not using us as a unit more often.

England was now on course for the championship. Two wins in a row may not sound like earth-shattering stuff, but it was seventeen years since England had won their opening two matches in the championship. I appreciated that captaining a national side was not always going to be as easy as this, but I thought I might as well enjoy it while the going was good.

Tony's superb match form had left us with a selection problem now that Mike Rafter was fit again. For the French game, should Tony keep his place or would it be better to revert to the combination that had started the season? Before the team was chosen, Sandy rang me up and asked what my recommendation would be. My reaction was to go for Tony. With the towering Bastiat at the tail of the French line-out, Tony was the man I needed. While Mike was more than capable, he lacked Tony's ability in terms of distribution, his quick thinking in awkward situations and, most important his undoubted line-out ability. I could take Bastiat out, but I could not guarantee the ball and wanted someone with skill in that department. Mike had never been that sort of a player. But I pointed out that Mike, for his part, had done more than most in the development of team spirit on and off the field, for which I, as skipper, was most grateful. But my vote went to Tony.

Sandy said he respected my opinion and would bear it in mind when it came to selection. That I was actually being asked what I thought was a great improvement: at last players and selectors seemed to be on the same wavelength. And this despite the fact that Budge Rogers, Mickey Weston, Malcolm Phillips and Derek Morgan all found their way into tracksuits to give Peter Colston a hand on the training field

In general, we had established some sort of rapport and the problems regarding lack of communication seemed to have been overcome to a large extent. But there was a hesitancy in Sandy's voice on the phone and his comments when Tony came into the side in Ireland had set me wondering. So when the team was announced, Tony's absence did not surprise me and I was personally disappointed that my views had been overruled, or rather ignored. Had they just been paying lip-service to my position? Sandy might respect my judgement, but he was not going to trust it.

Tony was not the only person to be rejected for England's match against France that year. Another to feel the sting of rejection was Norman Sanson, the Scottish referee. On the same day we trounced Scotland, Norman had been the centre of a controversial game between Wales and Ireland. Never one to stand any nonsense, he had sent off Wales's Geoff Wheel and Ireland's Willie Duggan for fighting. The press – normally very quick to demand that referees are right on the top of any trouble – crucified Norman, who without a shadow of a doubt was the best international official around. His dealings with players were always fair and his assessment of game situations was rarely wrong. Players knew exactly where they stood and he had the reputation of being a hard but consistent referee who would not be mucked about. His objectives on the field seemed to correspond with the players': he tried to let the game flow as much as possible and had an instinctive judgement of when to allow the advantage rule.

Norman had originally been a member of the Northumberland Referees Society before he came down south, so we saw quite a bit of him at Gosforth. Games seemed more enjoyable when he was in charge, more open and more flowing, although you were never left in any doubt that he would crack down on trouble immediately. So many referees see the eighty minutes as a battle between them and the players and believe that their main role is to try to impress their personality on the proceedings as much and as often as they can.

After that Cardiff match, Norman felt the full weight of the media boot in his groin. The relevant rugby unions, who knew that referees had been instructed that season to sort out any trouble on the field before it started, were guilty of abandoning their responsibility towards him. Norman characteristically kept quiet, though obviously he felt betrayed by many he thought had a similar attitude to the game. His one relief was that he had been picked to take charge of our game against France at Twickenham. At least that would present a quick return to the international fray, surely the best solution for all concerned.

He went to Paris to act as linesman for the game between France and Wales with fellow Scot Alan Hosie as referee. Immediately after that game, he was told his appointment as referee in the England match was not agreeable to the French; instead Jeff Kelleher would take charge. The news hit him hard; now he would have to wait for the next season to get back to where he belonged. Players, too, could not understand his shabby treatment and realized that it was not only players who were abused by the system and treated as second-class citizens by the rugby authorities.

Norman's absence put even more pressure on the man who took over. In just the same way, Tony Neary's absence meant that much was expected of our line-out man, Nigel Horton. The giant lock responded with one of his finest games in an England jersey, moving up and down the line-out to counter the threat of Bastiat. Once this French legend was shown to be a mere mortal, we stormed through to take control. Our domination, however, could not be turned into points and the

French sneaked back across the Channel with a 4 points to 3 victory on their way to only their second-ever Grand Slam. England's defeat was a real tragedy. Not only had Alastair Hignell missed five penalty attempts out of six, but several other scoring attempts were wasted. France were hardly in it and if we had put our noses in front, there is no doubt that they would have disappeared under our assault. But this season was meant to be different and not one of 'ifs' ...

When the game was drawing to its close and we were encamped near their line, we had been awarded a penalty. I signalled to Alastair to come up and have another go, but Nigel Horton was screaming at me to use the short penalty move they had devised at Moseley. Looking back, maybe I should have taken Nigel's advice; the French were tiring and it was possible that Nigel could have barged his way through. But I had remembered the mess we made of that tapped penalty against the French two years previously; surely, too the Flying Pig had to find his touch eventually. Near the end of an exhausting game my sluggish brain was not clicking through the many options as it should have been. Unfortunately, he missed and we never got close again. Still, hindsight is of little use to England now.

England's cause had not been helped when we lost Malcolm Young with a broken nose just after the interval. He should not have been so brave as he bundled Bastiat into touch to stop one of the French captain's barging runs.

Malcolm's departure did at least offer the opportunity of welcoming that *enfante terrible* Steve Smith back to the international scene. His introduction to the England side in 1973 had brought claims that he was our answer to Gareth Edwards. His commitment and concentration had wavered, and since that promising start he had been in and out of the side like a yo-yo. This French game initiated a brief return, but it was not until 1979 that he sorted himself out and at last did justice to his many talents. For that he can thank Fran Cotton, a big buddy from his Loughbrough College days. Fran provided him with the incentive to get himself back into shape for top-class rugby. In the early days, his expanding waistline and ample frame were often the source of comment

105

and amusement.

Malcolm was not the only one to be injured. Midway through the second half, someone caught me high up on the left-hand side of my back with his knee. The blow caused a haematoma, which created all sorts of spasms and put a severe strain on my lower back. By the end of the match, I was hobbling around because of the pain. Unfortunately, I thought it was just another knock and did not get a diagnosis immediately. This led to complications later on.

The injury only added to my sense of disappointment. Yet, although losing at this level is always unsatisfactory, this was our best showing of the season and continued the progress already made in earlier matches. In many ways, this was the first real sign of our new-found determination. The press reacted to the result in a similar fashion and we were all looking forward to the Triple Crown battle in Cardiff.

While annoyed at throwing away that winning start, we were still confident and we all believed that victory was well within our capabilities. Even further into the future, I was now being talked about as the likely British Lions' captain for the summer tour of New Zealand. The match in Wales would bring me into contact with my main rival for that post, fly-half Phil Bennett.

At one stage it looked as if that knock on my back might keep me out of the action. By the time I was home in Newcastle the back had seized up altogether and training was almost impossible. Eventually, I realized that I would need treatment and this meant missing the club game against Moseley the following Saturday. Now the Welsh challenge was only seven days away and I was desperate not to be absent. Luckily, the problem eased and I reported all-clear at Bristol on the Thursday for our preperations.

Our optimistic mood was infectious and nearly a thousand people turned up to watch us training at the Clere Club, Downend. Already that season, we had shown we could play rugby and had shown we could win away from home. I was convinced we could beat the Welsh in Cardiff at long last. For me, playing at Cardiff is like playing anywhere else.

It has been and will always be my contention that the

Welsh nation has done an absolutely superb job of fostering the notion that *hywl* is something peculiar to the Welsh, and to Cardiff in particular. That is an opinion that I do not share. All that it does is promote an over-the-top form of nationalistic pride in some people who don't really do any justice to the Welsh nation. I can remember vividly pausing momentarily just at the entrance to the field at Cardiff with spectators leaning over the side walls hurling down abuse and even spit. Fortunately, I have enough good memories of Welsh rugby to know that this was an isolated incident. But it has always stuck in my mind as a warning to these people and elements within the various countries who think winning is all-important.

In 1977 we were not being looked upon as lambs to the slaughter. Our record was impressive, and the Welsh defeat in Paris emphasized the great loss of Mervyn Davies. The legendary number eight who had been a certainty to lead the British Lions to New Zealand, had been struck down with a brain haemorrhage in Swansea's Welsh Cup semi-final match with Pontypool near the end of the previous season. There was no come-back from that, although fortunately Merv the Swerve made a complete recovery. His retirement was a bitter blow, not only for Welsh rugby but also the game in general. Wales were already struggling to replace probably the finest British forward since the Second World War. Jeff Squire had been tried for two matches, but was dropped for our visit. Geoff Wheel was back from suspension after that sending-off, so Derek Quinnell moved to number eight to join Clive Burgess and Trevor Evans in the back row. The Pontypool front row had to be split up when Charlie Faulkner withdrew through injury; Clive Williams came in to win his first cap.

Many saw this match as the ultimate examination of our standing within the European rugby community. Sadly, we failed that test, but fought gallantly before losing by 9 points to 14. Penalties from Alastair Hignell, who had a brilliant afternoon in defence, took us 6–0 and 9–7 in front, but we could not crack their solid defence. Instead, the man on whom so many of our attacks floundered, J.P.R. Williams struck again for his fifth try against England in six years.

My own day had been ruined by the flying doctor when I found out that my back was not as strong as I had thought. After a quarter of an hour, Wales won good scrum ball on our twenty-two-yard line and I stood off to cover in defence. My luck was out because I could see J.P.R. bearing down on me; I remember thinking that at last I would find out what tackling the great man was really like. A split second later I knew, and compared the experience to being hit by a brick wall. As he ploughed through me and I headed towards the ground, I felt my back go into involuntary spasms. The situation was nothing new to me, but, as before, the injury could not have happened at a more inconvenient time.

Receiving treatment, I told Peter Dixon that I would have to go off: the ideal cure for my condition was to lie down and relax with something warm on my back – the turmoil of the Arms Park was hardly the perfect place. Peter insisted that I stay on. The game was in its early stages and he said that my departure could be a psychological blow from which the rest of the boys might never recover.

What do you do in such a situation? Go or stay? Against my better judgement, I decided to stay and the rest of that match was one of the most frustrating experiences of my whole career. Three and a half years later, after a similar occasion, I made a different choice and left the big time for ever.

When something like your back goes, there are no outward signs of your disability – no cuts, bruises, bandages, or even that glazed look which signifies concussion. Instead, you slow up so badly that invariably you turn up in the wrong place at the wrong time ambling from bad to worse.

Geoff Wheel's return to the side gave the Welsh scrum a lot more solidity, while the English push was not helped by my weakness. This advantage in the scrum led to the opening Welsh try. We packed down for a scrum ten yards from our line and about fifteen yards in from touch, an ideal attacking position for Wales. We needed to disrupt possession somehow, but that proved an impossible task. We did not have the strength to push off the ball or the control to wheel the scrum. Our back row could not afford to stand off because then the Welsh scrum would have carried on its merry way right to our line for a pushover try. That meant that Peter Dixon, on the blind-side flank, had the impossible job of waiting for Gareth Edwards to make his move; from this sort of distance the scrum-half was lethal when he saw the line. By the time Peter saw Gareth break it was too late; even Mike Slemen, who decided to come in for the man in possession, was unable to prevent the Welsh terrier from diving over for yet another try against England. Although there was plenty of time to go, that try was the killer punch, demonstrating the Welsh power and superiority in an area where we had been expected to dominate. My presence on the field was certainly not helping England's cause.

Still, the pattern of many previous England visits to Cardiff was not repeated, and team did not grumble or crumble, and stuck to the job in hand right up to the final whistle. So, after such a promising start, we ended up with two wins out of four. Nigel Horton, who had been the hero a fortnight before, was only a shadow of the self he had been in France against the jumping Allan Martin. England had not carried on the promise of that French display.

The Welsh defeat ended my aspirations to the Lions captaincy. Up to that game I had been in front of Phil Bennett in most people's minds, but the pendulum swung heavily his way after his showing and the Welsh victory. My demise was based on my injury problems as much as anything else. I might have come through the South African campaign unscathed, but since then my career had been one long series of injuries, cry-offs, lay-offs and come-backs. I could well appreciate the selectors' fears that they could not rely on me staying injury-free for a three-month trek across New Zealand. The fact that I had stayed on the field looking below par made little difference to my case. If I had had to leave the field with a back injury, then the same sort of arguments would have applied.

I had a two-week wait for the party to be announced because there was another international Saturday before the selectors made up their minds. My back was not perfect, but Gosforth were on the cup trail again and there was no way I was going to miss out this time.

On the Monday after Wales had grabbed yet another Triple Crown at Murrayfield and France had collected their second Grand Slam in Dublin, the thirty names of those who would carry British hopes were announced. As expected Phil was made captain of the Lions party, which contained sixteen Welsh representatives. England provided six men, five of them forwards, a total that reflected our strength. Myself, Fran Cotton, Peter Wheeler, and Nigel Horton were included and there was also a place for Tony Neary, who had had a fine season with Lancashire. Peter Squires was our sole member of the back line and I knew he would be good company on the trip.

While not totally in agreement with Terry O'Connor's famous 'Too many Welshmen may spoil Lions' party' article in the *Daily Mail*, the squad did to me look a little top-heavy with men from the Principality, considering that Gareth Edwards, J.P.R. Williams and Gerald Davies were unavailable. Other withdrawals included Fergus Slattery and Peter Dixon, who never went on a major tour after the 1971 British Lions visit to New Zealand.

I was examined by the Lions doctor Gordon Rowley, who pronounced me healthy enough to tour, although I felt the fitness cloud was still hanging over my head. The Scottish contingent pointed to two glaring omissions and I was surprised there was no room for Jim Renwick, who had been showing his best form, and Ian McLauchlan, who had forced his way back into the national side and whose experience would have proved invaluable. But the tour was six weeks away; I put it to the back of my mind and concentrated my energies on Gosforth's cup run.

A controlled performance, very typical of Gosforth at the time, took us past London Welsh in Richmond into the John Player Cup Final yet again. That success over Welsh opposition at least offered some consolation to Peter, Malcolm and myself for that Cardiff failure.

A week before the final, the offer of another Barbarians tour proved irresistible, especially as the Cardiff match gave me the opportunity of packing down in the back row with Jean-Pierre Rives and Jean-Claude Skerla, a pair of Frenchmen who were among the most exciting flankers in the world. We won, too, and then enjoyed another leisurely day on the golf course. But the Barbarians jinx struck again for the second time that season, as I was enjoying lunch before the Swansea match. Not for the first time, mealtime was the occasion of an Uttley seizure. My back went into spasms ... what with my three-minute performance against Leicester, Geoff Windsor Lewis was showing great patience. Andy Ripley thought it rather bad form having to play at such short notice.

Fortunately, the spasms relented to allow me an appearance in the final; there was no way I was going to spend my cup final as club captain again watching the boys win the cup, from a position in the stand. The game coincided with a family wedding down in Wales, so I drove Kris, her parents and young Simon down to Bristol and caught the train back to London to join up with the lads.

It will be of no surprise to any of you to hear I was consorting with Doctor Leo after only a few minutes of the action. Some wayward Waterloo boot had caught me behind the ear and I had to go off to be stitched up. Consequently, the rest of the first half went by rather hazily, though I had recovered sufficiently to appreciate David Robinson racing in for a couple of tries just after the interval. Waterloo never recovered from that double blow and we ran in a total of five tries for a 27 points to 11 victory.

Gosforth were really on song that day; I found the style of rugby invigorating to play because we tried to embrace everyone. Some complained that it wasn't pretty to watch and that the side played like fifteen forwards. Apart from anything else, though, we were effective and delighted to be told that if we won the cup for a third time the following year, the club could keep it. Unfortunately, our treble failed and the trophy is now the proud possession of Leicester, who won it outright in 1981 when they, ironically, overcame Gosforth in the final.

The only drawback for me that day was that I had to leave almost immediately and head back to Bristol. Swathed in bandages, my appearance on the Inter-City 125 brought some strange looks. The only piece of news that cheered me up

111

about missing the celebrations was hearing that Steve Gustard left the banquet with a bottle of scotch and, in his own inimitable style, had managed to fall over in the corridor, land on the bottle and cut his backside to ribbons. It couldn't have happened to a nicer fellow! After our victory, I tried to put everything that had happened to me that season into perspective. With England's showing in the championship and the Lions selection I had been so near and yet so far; but there was still plenty to achieve. With this major expedition to All Black country, I felt at the beginning of a great adventure. Little did I imagine that my career would come to an abrupt end in the space of the next few weeks.

8

'You'll Never Play Again'

I never made that Lions tour and, of course, my back was the reason. The seeds of my destruction had been sown with that bang during the French game. The late diagnosis of the haematoma had led to a frantic ten days of osteopathic and acupuncture treatment before that Welsh international. Even today, I'm not sure whether I did the right thing by playing against Wales. Was it an error of judgement? I remember that Ian McLauchlan did the same sort of thing when he played against us in 1973, three weeks after breaking a leg against Ireland. His side lost that day and Mighty Mouse was held to blame. Like him, I was captain and like him I faced plenty of criticism after defeat.

My back had not been restricting my normal activities and on the Thursday before the Wales match I got through the training session without too much difficulty. Maybe I was kidding myself about being 100 per cent fit. My presence as captain was as important as it was as player and I think this swayed me into taking a calculated risk. Not that such a situation is unusual. There is seldom an international match takes place these days without several players being less than fully fit; painkilling injections are increasingly becoming the order of the day. It is one of the hazards of a crowded championship season and an amateur game. Unfortunately, the chance of running into J.P.R. was something I couldn't insure against and when that happened my calculated risk became a gamble that had failed. The reasons for remaining on the field have been explained in the previous chapter, but the decision did neither me, my back nor England any favours.

There was an article in the following Monday's *Daily Express* by Tony Bodley, claiming that I should not have been playing in the first place. The story quoted Sandy Sanders as saying that I should have withdrawn knowing I wasn't 100 per cent fit. That didn't sound like Sandy and he confirmed his version of the affair in a letter to me. The place of his interview had been the foyer of the crowded Centre Hotel immediately after the game. He was asked whether I should have played if I knew I was not up to the task. This was hardly the environment for a lengthy discussion and Sandy merely replied that I was obviously feeling the injury.

The secretary of the RFU, Bob Weighill, also received a copy of Sandy's letter and then got in touch with the sports editor of the *Daily Express* to complain about his correspondent's lack of factual reporting. Bob sent me a letter informing me of what he had done.

Sandy has very kindly sent me a copy of the letter which he wrote to you on March 7th, regarding the article which appeared in Monday's *Daily Express*. As you can well imagine we are all disgusted by the article and I have made this view known to the sports editor of the *Daily Express* and I have also made it known to him that we have lost confidence in the ability of his rugby writer to report factually and accurately and in keeping with the mood and spirit of personal relationships within Rugby Football. I wholeheartedly support what Sandy has written and say that you have succeeded in raising England's rugby out of the doldrums and creating a tremendous upsurge in interest throughout the whole country. This can only be achieved by the superb leadership which has been apparent from President through chairman of selectors and to the person who matters most on the field of play, the captain of the England XV.

He signed off 'yours ever', which was rather ironic because a month later my contribution to England's revival was held in rather less regard by one and the same Bob Weighill. The argument was over the payment of medical bills for the treatment I had incurred in getting fit for the game against Wales. The intensive work on my back came to about £90 and, as I had done in the past when getting in shape for England, I sent the bills through to Don Rutherford.

114

He passed them on to Bob Weighill, who sent me a letter:

Don Rutherford has passed me your letter and the various medical accounts which you have received for treatment over the past few months. I do not believe that these accounts can be entirely the responsibility of the RFU and I have approached Gosforth with the suggestion that the fees that have been paid to the club over the past few months as a result of your various BBC interviews could be used for this purpose.

This time his communication was signed 'yours sincerely'. I rang him up to find out why the RFU could not see their way to settling these amounts. If they did, Bob told me, then everyone would be jumping on the bandwagon and claiming treatment off the union. This took me aback slightly: it was for England's benefit, as well as my own, that I had spent many hours on the treatment couch. I was very lucky that the school authorities were so generous in allowing me time off. Bob again brought up the BBC money that had been paid to the club in order to retain my amateur status. This struck me as unfair because it was for England, and not Gosforth, that the treatment was undertaken. Anyway, my England duties and various injuries had meant the club had seen very little of me in a Gosforth jersey that season.

The affair annoyed me for two reasons. Firstly, because all my fight to regain full fitness had been for England. Secondly, and more upsetting, there was the implication that Gosforth had been repaying the money back to me that I had given them from the BBC. I resented that. Furthermore, the money paid to a club or union in this manner, is not for use like a bank deposit account to be drawn on by the players when they needed it. I added that if the money had been paid into the RFU Charitable Trust would they now be responsible for my medical expenses? The final insult to the man who had 'raised England's rugby out of the doldrums', to quote the words of Bob himself, came when I pointed out that, with the whole matter becoming rather sordid, I did not think it too much to expect the RFU to settle this bill. The current captain of England was then put firmly in his place as Bob informed me, 'A lot of people want to be captain of England.

115

You are not indispensible, you know. Anyway, there's always someone else wanting to step into your shoes.'

My usefulness and privileged position were fast becoming a thing of the past.

That treatment only signalled the beginning of my back troubles. In the early stages, the problem didn't seem too serious. Even pulling out of that Barbarians match did not cause me much concern and my departure from the John Player final had nothing to do with my back. After that match, I made the big mistake of using the three weeks before the tour began as a rest period. Although nothing was troubling me, those three weeks contained no rugby nor any training.

The weekend after the final, I found myself involved in mountain rescue. The instigator of this exercise was Peter Roberts, with whom I had been in college; he was looking for a celebrity to drag up and down the Cheviots in a survival bag; and I was the mug who accepted. Being strapped to a stretcher and hauled about all afternoon didn't help my back at all.

This, combined with total inactivity, was my big mistake. The muscles in my back got out of tone and as a result all sorts of problems arose in my lumbar regions. The root of all my trouble was an extra vertebra, which left my back a vulnerable area. As well as not training in this run-in to the tour, I was also not receiving any treatment – not for reasons of finance, but because I did not think I needed it. I thought that once I was back training then the benefit of this lay-off would be considerable.

After saying goodbye to Kris and Simon, who was now thirteen months, I travelled down to London with Peter Squires to join the tour party. Our first port of call was the White Elephant Club on the Thames for the Rugby World Player of the Year award luncheon. Not surprisingly, Phil Bennett had beaten me to it yet again and I had to make do with the runner's-up award: yet another tankard, but at least it held an impressive two pints of liquid.

After the luncheon, we all assembled at Richmond and our venture was under way. I thought that it was important to straighten out a few things with Phil Bennett before the tour started. Although we had been the main contenders for the captaincy, I explained that any rivalry between us was over as far as I was concerned and that I would give him all the help I could over the next three and a half months.

Our training started the following day, Saturday, at Twickenham. My back felt stiff as I changed, but I expected it to ease out with a bit of exercise. Unfortunately, the longer the session went on, the more restricted my movements became. During a passing session with Steve Fenwick, I noticed that bending, especially, was difficult. Be careful, I thought, or this tour will end before it had begun. A long soak in a hot bath brought no relief and the now-familiar feeling of panic came over me as I was getting dressed. We changed into our number two outfit for the team photograph behind the west stand. Sitting in the front row between Gordon Brown and Fran Cotton, I felt decidedly uncomfortable.

On the bus back to the hotel, the pain was so bad that I couldn't sit down. There was still time for the situation to clear itself up so, for the time being, I kept the bad news to myself, half leaning on the arm of one of the seats on the coach and trying to look as nonchalant as possible in the circumstances. As luck would have it, the booking arrangements gave me a room to myself.

By keeping quiet, I was not trying to deceive anybody, just hoping to buy enough time for the pain to depart to allow me on the plane. As yet, there was no idea in my mind that I might miss the tour, although I was conscious that any snap decision by the selectors, already worried about my past history, might count against me. That afternoon I stretched out on the bed to watch the rugby league cup final. Lying down or standing did not present too many problems, but trying to sit down had become a nightmare.

The Four Home Union Tours Committee held their farewell dinner that night and the occasion only added to my discomfort. A suggestion by Derek Quinnell for an early night temporarily saved my bacon and we took a cab back to Richmond. As I got into bed that night, I knew tomorrow would be a day of decision and that I would have to share my sob story with somebody else. Any prayers that night concerned my back. They had not been answered when I awoke the next morning. I didn't even have to get out of bed to know that my back was worse and that there was no chance of me spending thirty-six hours on a plane to New Zealand.

My distress call went to Doctor Leo and he came to my room about 8.30 a.m. Despite my casual phone message – 'I may have a little problem' – the situation was quickly diagnosed as far more serious. The tour management – Dod Burrell and John Dawes – were quickly called and Leo also contacted an orthopaedic consultant friend of his. My room soon became like a private ward in 'General Hospital'. A prolapsed disc was the experts' verdict and the consultant thought it might take me some time to recover. My own previous experience was that a few days in bed might see me right.

What was agreed was that I was in no fit state to undertake a strenuous flight. The group huddled together and I was asked whether I thought I would be fit to travel in a fortnight's time. Yes, was my reply, although I couldn't guarantee anything. This time the group went outside for their discussions and deliberations. I knew they were deciding my fate; the tension was unbearable and I was very quickly coming round to the idea that I was about to cease being a 1977 British Lion. Then Sid (as we knew John Dawes) came back into the room: 'If you are fit to travel in a fortnight's time, then we'd like you to join the party in New Zealand.'

Maybe my prayers had been answered after all. Sid was my main saviour; when we had first assembled, he said he was looking forward to us working together and hoped he had my cooperation. Of course, he had, especially after this reprieve.

With a stay of execution, the feeling of panic disappeared. The rest of Sunday I spent lazing around while the lads went to a reception at New Zealand House. They were to leave London on Tuesday, but I returned to Newcastle on Monday. That short flight was the final proof that attempting to get on a plane to New Zealand would have been folly. Saying goodbye to the players I remembered my similar experience before England's tour of South Africa in 1972: the same embarrassed looks, the lowered heads and the mumbled commiserations. My comments to Phil Bennett about being able to rely on me were looking rather foolish.

Home in Newcastle an appointment was made for me to see David Stainsby, a top orthopaedic consultant in the north. In the light of my past experiences and his medical opinion, bed rest seemed the best solution to the problem. I was put through various tests to show just how restricted my movements were; when my two weeks grace were up, then I should return to David and a final decision would be taken.

Lying in bed never really bothered me; if I'm honest, I enjoy nothing better than reading and listening to the radio. The time seldon dragged. My welfare was of great concern to a wealth of people, media and otherwise. Letters arrived daily with details of miracle cures and traditional remedies from other back sufferers. One such 'witch doctor' was a Welshman called Wyndom Thomas, who worked for the National Coal Board and had come up to Gateshead on business.

He popped into see me – after first dropping in to the local paper to inform it of his impending visit. His 'cure' was based on the idea that you had to pump yourself full of vitamin C, which would help the regeneration of cells. I only tried it once and it brought me out in a hot flush. But he was a very interesting bloke and I was grateful that people were taking time and trouble to try and help me.

Unfortunately, time was running out and the sad truth was becoming more inescapable with every dawn; sleep was fast becoming my hope for a miracle cure. This was not my normal back trouble but something far more serious. Some mornings would see an improvement, but it would only be one step forward to take two steps back later in the day.

Reading the details of the opening Lions matches, my interest began to wane when it became obvious I was not going to be able to join then. D-Day was 19 May, a Friday, only fourteen days after the Lions had assembled in London; then my only problem had been about how we were going to beat the All Blacks. Kris drove me down to Nutfield Hospital where I was to try the various tests again. Only one exercise was necessary to tell me what I already knew. For this test, lying on your back you have to raise a straight leg up; you should be able to reach right angles to the ground. I managed a meagre 15 degree lift. Like my confrontation with Leo Walden during my fitness test for England's South African tour, the test was merely a gesture. It was a relief to have the matter settled once and for all, although I would have dearly loved to be on that plane to face the All Blacks.

I had to ring John Lawrence, the secretary of the Four Home Unions Tours Committee, to tell him that I would not be making it to New Zealand. John said he was sorry and we exchanged a few pleasantries. Jeff Squire went instead and I sent him a telegram wishing him all the best.

My future no longer revolved around the Lions; now there was the small question of getting fit for life in general. Bed rest was obviously not the answer, so David Stainsby suggested a period of traction.

Those ten days in traction were a real ordeal. My condition and temper deteriorated rapidly. The mere mechanics of the treatment leave you feeling like an absolute cripple. I was placed on an inclined bed with a harness around my waist that had ropes down the side and weights on the end. A real instrument of torture. Very quickly the pressure from the weights caused a deadening of the nerve in my thighs and slowly any sensation of feeling went. Not only was my condition not improving, but I could feel the strength draining out of me as I became as weak as a kitten. Constipation did not help my state of mind either; even when I was wheeled around on my portable commode to a place of satisfaction, the mere act of moving my bowels was an exhausting exercise. But there were compensations. One day with the sun streaming into the ward, Kris arrived at visiting time and there, staggering alongside her for his first steps in my presence, was Simon; a very special moment.

That apart, this was a miserable period; there could be no denying the complete failure of this treatment in my case. David Stainsby was rather depressed as he explained that he had now investigated all avenues open to him, other than an operation. Back surgery is very risky and he was reluctant to take this final solution.

David added that if I wanted a second opinion, I should feel free to obtain one. Such action would not be treated as a snub and he would look forward to seeing me again should the alternatives prove fruitless. My progress so far had not been what either of us had hoped or wanted, but I was extremely grateful for all he had done and for leaving the door open for future consultation.

While suffering under the traction, one of the more sensible-sounding letters I received was from a local chiropractor called Peter Lomax. A chiropractor tries to cure by manipulation of the joints, especially those of the spine. Peter was just setting up his practice and, as success with such a lame duck as me, would be a considerable boost to his reputation, his treatment was offered free of charge. Now I was on my own, this was an important consideration; with my playing days fast disappearing into the background, I could not justify medical expenses to club or county and it was unlikely that the RFU would receive any request from me favourably after our recent discussion over money matters.

The failure of conventional methods had had a disheartening effect on me and I was relieved when Peter's treatment eased my condition. The whole process was alarmingly slow. At long last car-driving came within the scope of my capabilities and made life much less restricting.

The Lions were coming up to the first test and BBC radio was putting on a 'Test Match Special' programme linking up rugby clubs in England, Wales, Scotland and Ireland. The basic idea was to keep everybody awake until the live commentary of the game, which would start about four in the morning. But, because the match was also being televised the following morning, many people wanted to watch it on the box without knowing the result. Ian Robertson and I had been at Gosforth organizing that line-up from seven o'clock the previous evening, so it was a very long night indeed. The programme nevertheless contained many funny moments, as you would expect with personalities like Willie John McBride, Syd Millar, Carwyn James, Ian McLauchlan, Bill McLaren, with Cliff Morgan and Terry Wogan in London. But the proposal to cover all four internationals in a similar manner was abandoned; as well as the competition from television the Lions went tumbling to defeat that first night.

My public appearances increased that summer, as I became Tyne Tees TVs rent-a-celebrity. Before I took up duties there, I appeared with Fiona Johnston on BBC's 'Look North' cookery programme. I don't think Robert Carrière was watching, but I'm sure he would have been impressed with my steak and chips, rugby-style. Later I was the resident chairman for the panel of judges which was choosing Miss Tyne Tees 1977. The competition was run over several weeks and was compered by Derek Batey of 'Mr and Mrs' fame.

Even in the midst of all these beauties, I managed to put my size 12 feet right in it. After the final we all moved upstairs for a reception in the hospitality room and I found myself talking to the overjoyed girl who had just won. The competition was decided on the number of votes contestants received from each individual judge; it was possible to win without being placed first by any of the judges, which is in fact what had happened on this occasion. On congratulating the winner, my comments had this unintended sting in their tail: 'You did well considering none of us put you in first place.' Well, as you can imagine, my revelation went down like a lead balloon and left the girl rather distressed.

That incident apart, those programmes were thoroughly enjoyable and offered some compensation for missing the tour. My journey to television 'stardom' continued with a BBC 'Look North' quiz programme when I made up the sports panel with Bobby Moncur and Brendan Foster.

My back kept me off school for ten weeks and I returned in July, only a few weeks before the summer holidays began. My progress was agonizingly slow and, although I was able to lead a normal life in a subdued sort of way, there looked little chance of me playing any rugby at all, let alone leading England. To deteriorate from being so physically fit and active to – in my eyes – the state of a cripple was cruelly frustrating. Decorating became the order of the day that summer, as long as I didn't mind putting up with an aching back for a couple of hours or so. My condition had stabilized:

no better, no worse, just a form of stalemate. John Elders kindly lent us his caravan and we managed a holiday in Ripon before spending a few days with my folks in Blackpool. The sun and fresh air got to me as it always does and I ran a mile and a half back from the beach to the house in bare feet.

The aftereffects of this foolishness showed just how weak I had become and the experience impressed on me just how poor my condition was. All the swimming I had put in had helped, but I was a long way from my old self. So it was back to David Stainsby in the middle of August to keep an appointment for a progress report. He agreed there was some improvement, but also agreed that I had not improved enough. Taking care was still the order of the day and my condition seemed to have reached some sort of plateau. Again the back operation was mentioned, this time as a serious alternative. As a preliminary to an operation, I would have to undergo a mylogram X-ray, which ascertains what damage there is and how it can be mended.

On the same day as these discussions took place, the British Lions returned home having lost the test series 1–3, a poignant reminder of what might have been. For me at this stage, rugby – any rugby – still looked an impossible dream.

The investigative X-ray was fixed for the following week. It is a complicated affair and not very pleasant. I was strapped to a table on my stomach and then dye was injected into my lower spine; this would show up all the disc spaces and nerve supply. In order to get the dye flowing, I was rotated vertically around 180 degrees on this table. Probably the worst aspect of the test is that you can see yourself on a monitor, with the dye moving within your spine. By contorting your back, you can distort the dye and control its movements in a small way; these images help you actually to feel the dye in your back.

Because the treatment can give you severe headaches, I was kept in hospital for twenty-four hours, a normal precaution. These headaches may be caused by the extra pressure on the spine when the patient sits up and the dye flows back down; the effect of the rotating table may also be a cause. Initially this big tough rugby player had no ill-effects; I read and then stayed up late to watch the television. After a couple of hours' sleep, though, I woke up feeling absolutely awful, worse than from any hangover. I had just about settled down by the time Kris picked me up the next morning. But after the motion of the car journey home – no reflection on Kris's driving I must add – I was sick on arrival and had to go to bed.

The report from the mylogram was ready the following week so I went to see the consultant neurologist at the general hospital. His room on the top floor of that department reminded me that my disability was not so bad after all. Here were people who had been left so badly affected by strokes and congenital neurological problems that I almost felt ashamed, something of a fake. I might not be fit enough for top-class sport, but in terms of life as an individual, it was an insult to bring my problems into the same room as these people. So often we are so wrapped up in our own troubles that we need a sharp jolt to realize that the world does not revolve around our own axis. The consultant's report was encouraging. My back was not in great shape, but it also was not in a serious enough state to merit an operation which might easily make matters worse. So he came to the conclusion that there was nothing clinically he could do for my condition.

Where did that leave me? Without rugby, was the implication – one which I had gradually come to terms with over the summer months as I slowed down a notch or two. It was difficult not to resent the fact that my sporting career had been snatched away from me just when it was taking off. Retiring early through injury was something I had always supposed happened to other players, not me.

Shortly after, Kris and I came down to London for the Queen's Silver Jubilee match between the Barbarians and the British Lions. Really, I wasn't yet over the upset or able to come to terms with my disability so, after a weekend of feeling out of it, I decided to keep away from the rugby scene until I was more settled in my mind.

At least now I could devote my energies to Cramlington and my teaching duties; about time, too – after all, I'd been there five years and, although I did not know it at the time, this was my final term in teaching.

With a back operation impractical, David Stainsby thought that regular physiotherapy and remedial exercise might be the answer. Norman Anderson, a physio lecturer at Newcastle Polytechnic, was the man he suggested I see; his track record with Brendan Foster, David Jenkins and other international athletes was impressive and, as ever, I had nothing to lose. Unfortunately, Norman wasn't the answer for me, but he was a great character; as broad as he was tall, he subsequently became involved with the Northumberland county side. His tunnel vision caused a great moment of hilarity during the 1978–79 county championship final at Twickenham, where we met Middlesex. His services were required during a break in the action, so on he belted at top speed only for his restricted view to bring him to the wrong group of players as he vainly searched for someone in need of attention. When he eventually arrived at his correct destination, I suggested that it might be time he obtained a homing device.

Such joking was in the future. Humour was a commodity in rare supply in my life at the time; my lack of progress was beginning to get me down, especially as my condition remained static. Norman had helped me psychologically, though, as he impressed the need for hard work. But rugby – at least playing it – was over and I had to start thinking about my life outside sport. Coincidentally, it was around this time that an offer to work outside teaching came up. Geoffrey Windsor Lewis, the Barbarians secretary, told me at the Gosforth centenary dinner of an opportunity in the sports trade. The company was AMF, an American concern that was run in the UK by none other than Roger Arneil, the man who had led us into forward battle against the Springboks in 1969. We met and agreed terms, so I was able to hand in my notice at Cramlington that half-term. This would release me to work for Roger in January.

Leaving the school was a wrench, especially as the first lot of kids I had taken through were now in the sixth form. One of the parting gifts I received from the kids was a Snoopy picture mirror with the inscription, 'Isn't it great to be a superstar'. Well, I didn't feel like one at the time, I can tell you.

Had it not been for my back, I might have remained in teaching. But times had changed and so had my circumstances; I had to change with them. Yet, the move was fortuitous; my life today has its roots in that switch and it also, indirectly, led me back onto the rugby field.

9

Captain of England, Again

Ironically, my eventual cure came from one of the many weird and wonderful postal communications I was still receiving. That they were all, to the letter you might say, read with great care and attention is evidence of my desperation and belief that somewhere might be a grain of hope that would turn into a cure for me. The author of this particular correspondence was well known to me. Jeff Butterfield, still remembered as England's finest centre since the Second World War, now runs the Rugby Club in London's Hallam Street.

He told me that one of his club members, a physiotherapist, had helped international footballer Gerry Francis to recovery after a back injury. Gerry's story was very similar to mine. Both of us had been captain of England before injury ended our brief period in the limelight. Jeff had spoken to the physio, who thought he might be able to help me. What Terry Moule was not was a physiotherapist – a point he made most forcibly in a letter a couple of days later – he was in fact a naturopath osteopath; notwithstanding, he reiterated Jeff's offer of help. If I was ever in the area, then I was to look in. While keen to look anywhere for hope, the long tedious months of little progress had made me sceptical and cynical of all assertions.

I decided to get in touch with Gerry Francis as the simplest way of checking the claims of Jeff and Terry, to find out exactly what had been wrong with him and how Terry had helped. Gerry had been on the point of real success, which would have meant for him, as a professional sportsman, a small fortune. From his brief description, his problem sounded worse than mine; he agreed that Terry had been a big help and suggested that I give him a go.

This I did in November 1977. The treatment was not the immediate cure which I had always hoped for but which experience had taught me never to expect. Terry's healing process was based on the neuro-muscular technique invented by Stanley Lief, a Russian Jew who had emigrated to the United States before settling in England. The object is, with the pressure of the fingers and thumbs, to break down soft-tissue lesions and muscle abnormalities so that the bones when corrected can function properly. Terry's first session brought some relief, but by the time I got back home to Newcastle from Hemel Hempstead the benefits had worn off. It seemed such a long way to go for just a dream. Terry Moule might have been the answer for Gerry Francis, but the Uttley back would beat even him. Had I not gone to work for AMF, based in Oxford and within striking distance of Terry's Hemel practice, then our paths might have drifted apart as easily as they crossed, and without any real benefits to either side.

Once regular sessions became the norm, however, his treatment began to have a real effect and my condition improved steadily ... which was just as well because I was discovering the hard way about the pressures and turmoil of being a travelling salesman. The easy-going environment of teaching seemed part of a different world as I clocked up 50,000 miles in my first year on the road. The sales area I had to cover was extensive, to say the least – from the Severn to the Wash and northwards. My placid temperament wasn't exactly suited to the hard-selling aggressive techniques expected. Fortunately, many of the shop owners knew me and gave orders to help me out.

Some areas of my patch I knew too well. How could I go into a sports shop in South Shields and convince the owner that he needed a dozen expensive tennis racquets when I knew the only tennis courts in a four-mile radius were a couple of derelict playgrounds with no nets and covered in potholes. Perhaps I understood their plight too well. When it came to the big pressure sell, my efforts and heart were less committed. But, despite being on average about three nights away and despite the loneliness of plastic hotels, I found motoring through the beautiful Scottish countryside was a great compensation and a reminder of my days at college.

Slowly and surely, Terry was putting me back together. Even touching my knees had been a problem in the old days. Playing again had become a possibility and not just a pipedream, but my career switch would make fitting in senior rugby very difficult. As yet, anyway, the return was only a suggestion. Having come to terms with life without rugby, life at a more leisurely pace, I was careful not to set my sights too high. It could so easily lead to further disappointments and failures. I wasn't convinced that I wanted to take that chance or that I would be able to cope with the consequences. It might be a lot easier if I just left things the way they were.

As my condition improved, though, I seemed to be slowly enticed back into rugby circles. My television career continued when I went to Murrayfield to help Bill McLaren with his commentary on the Calcutta Cup match. Not that Bill needed any help. His preparations and homework before a game are legendary; sitting with him that afternoon was a real insight, a chance to see one of television's top commentators at work.

England played well that day to win, having started the season with two defeats; David Caplan, making his debut at full-back, looked a fine prospect. I joined up with the boys for post-match drinks at the North British; although everybody seemed pleased to see me, I suddenly felt a bit of an intruder, not only on their own territory but on my own past. I made my apologies and slipped quietly away, then spent the car journey back to Newcastle in nostalgic thought.

Although my serious challenge on the rugby world would have to wait until the following season, I did make one appearance at the tail end of the 1977–78 season. My name appeared at the top of the list for an International fifteen that played Cockermouth Select at Laithwaite on 16 April, a year to the day since I had lifted the John Player Cup aloft at Twickenham. Dave Robinson was the organizer of the match and he approached me to see if I was interested in a game. I wasn't sure, but when he saw me wavering he dangled the carrot of the full-back spot in front of me. We who play in the scrum have always had delusions of grandeur and so, perhaps against my better judgement, there I was pulling on the number fifteen jersey. The atmosphere in the dressing room, even for a Sunday game, really got me going again. Just being able to bend down and tie up my boots after all this time was a great feeling, especially as I was surrounded with plenty of old friends, like Tony Neary and Fran Cotton. Gosforth's Brian Patrick was shunted out to the wing to make room for this returning relic. I might have showed a few deft touches, but I don't think he ever worried that his regular spot might be in danger. The season was drawing to a close and this experiment was merely an aside. Simon, despite himself, had reached his second birthday in March, and on 25 April Benjamin Adam Uttley arrived. Family life and business ambitions were my chief concerns now.

Terry's treatment had given me the confidence to take part in a 'fun run' around Newcastle's Town Moor during one of the bank holiday weekends. Malcolm Young and I were worried when the international athlete Mike McLeod joined us at the start. But he was just out for a loosener and so we felt safe enough to trot round around with him. Henry Cooper was the official starter as we set off on our mile and a half run. By the end of that distance I had eased up enough to actually bend down and touch my toes, something I had not accomplished for eighteen months. By next morning my back had tightened up again, but little by little I was getting better.

Terry never let me forget that his ultimate aim was to put me back on the rugby field. I wasn't so sure, but his positive thinking was an important aid to my recovery. Suddenly, the summer was over and I had to decide whether to leave well alone or to give rugby another go. Here I was, nearly twenty nine years of age, a former captain of England with seventeen caps, as well as being a British Lions test player, with a young family and a new job. Was it fair to them to take such a risk. Probably not, but I felt I owed it to everyone who had helped me since my injury to prove that I could at least get through eighty minutes of rugby. But the real reason, if I was totally honest, was that I wanted one more crack at the big time again.

My comeback began in August at the Kelvinside Sevens in Glasgow. It was hardly Twickenham, but it was a start. Propping for Gosforth that afternoon was my first competitive game since that 1977 John Player Cup final. It was a pleasant afternoon, enhanced by the company of the Patrick brothers in the side, and, although we didn't win anything, my official return to rugby had taken place without any hitches.

The whisper had already gone out that England's forgotten man was beginning the long road back. I would have preferred to have remained fairly inconspicuous until I really knew whether I was physically capable of mounting a serious challenge for my old Gosforth place; my ambitions were no higher than that. Terry suggested, and I agreed, that a couple of games for Hemel Hempstead might be the answer. My presence, we hoped, would not attract too much attention and I should be able to keep out of any trouble at this level. Should I find myself in any difficulties with my back, then Terry was on hand.

The telephone wires had remained torturingly quiet since my withdrawal from the Lions tour. During the two weeks' grace I was given when my back injury first flared up, the media concern almost put me on a par with royalty. Then ... silence. Now the word was out again, and the telephone started buzzing. 'How are things?' 'What are your expectations?' Trying not to be cynical, I appreciated the job they had to do. When you are 'in', there's no end to their attention, when you are 'out', it's spelt with a capital S for solitary.

Quite a few of the famous rugby press turned up for my debut against Leighton Buzzard, but I felt no pressure and was going to take things how they came. Only a few steps onto the field told me how I had missed playing yet I tried not to be carried away on this wave of emotion because there was no way physically that I could cope with any major confrontation. At the first breakdown, I looked up to see the familiar face of Stuart Maxwell in Leighton's colours. Stuart, formerly of New Brighton and Richmond, was the winger who had scored two tries that sank the All Blacks at Warrington in

1972. He was the brother of England centre Andy Maxwell, whose career had been ended by a serious knee injury in the international in Paris earlier that year.

'What the hell are you doing here?' I inquired. He said that he could just as easily ask me the same question. Communications were halted until we met in the bar, but it was quite a relief to see somebody I knew, even though he was on the other side.

My return was not completely injury free – somebody stood on my big toe. Don't laugh, the pain was excruciating and affected everything else; even my back began to ache. The newspaper headline writers would have had a field day if England's former captain had broken down on his debut because someone had stood on his foot!

At least I held my place for the following week! Peter Lomax, who wanted to meet Terry, came down for the game, but I don't think the pair hit it off too well. Peter is rather an introverted type while Terry has all the confidence of the south. As I came through my second test, Peter had to admit that Terry had done the trick. Now I was convinced that I might be able to stand up to the rigours of top-class rugby again and so made myself available for Gosforth.

Was I doing the right thing? For a start, training and keeping fit was no longer an easy task. While I had been a teacher of PE, I was normally in very good shape, as I could take as much exercise as I wanted. Life on the road was a completely different proposition and I had to snatch training opportunities where and when I could fit them in. When I was at home, Gosforth was my destination but a lot of the time I was away from home, This meant I appeared at Moseley, Gordonians in Aberdeen, Purley in Surrey, West of Scotland, and Roundhay, when the Yorkshire squad were assembled, at various times during the season. Being used to regular exercise in the past, I did not find the new arrangements totally satisfying, but I had made my career choice, and would have to make the best of it.

After that trial run at Hemel, my career suddenly took off at a tremendous pace, much quicker than I wanted it to. Even today, it still frightens me when I think I was back in an

England jersey less than ten weeks after my debut for Hemel. I might have recovered some of my form, but there was no way that my body strength and recovery rate were good enough for rugby at this level after such a short spell of time. Ultimately, I was to pay the penalty for all this early haste.

My first game back for Gosforth was in the first fifteen and we travelled to do battle with Broughton Park. Opposite me at the tail of the line-out was the familiar face of Tony Neary. He smiled. 'Nice to see you back!' Yet his actions over the next eighty minutes made me wonder if I had done the right thing as he showed me how much I had still to make up.

As each obstacle was overcome, my philosophy of treating every game as a bonus made me very optimistic about my playing future. The Argentinians were making an early-season tour of England, but even I resisted the selectors' advances and avoided a really speedy return to representative honours. Such haste would have been madness. As it was, I was wearing a Northumberland jersey only a month after appearing back for Gosforth, as the county set off to try and win the Northern title. My timing was perfect; in a vintage season, we faced Lancashire in the final game with everything to play for. If we won by a single point, then Lancashire would win the title but if we were successful by three points or more, then Northumberland would take the Northern title for the first time since 1970. If we won by two points, then confusion would follow, but that was unlikely. We seemed home and dry with a 12 points to 6 lead until, in the very last minute of the match, Tony Neary reduced the deficit. Everything was now hanging on David Gullick's conversion, but even when he hooked that final kick of the afternoon, we still weren't sure if we had won the title. We had by 0.090969 of a point – although the arguments raged well on into the night.

That weekend carried even more significance because the Midlands met the All Blacks the same day and immediately afterwards the selectors were to announce the England side to meet New Zealand at Twickenham the following Saturday. The selectors were keeping an eye on me and a lot of people were predicting that I would be back in the side. As for myself,

after such a short spell back I was not sure I was yet ready –
physically or mentally – for the rigours of the international
arena. Nevertheless, when the team was named, there I was at
number eight and I was delighted, although the team as a
whole came under plenty of criticism. 'Mad', 'inconsistent',
and 'awful' were just a few of the adjectives flying about and
most of the disagreement centred on the choice of the front
five. The back row, of Peter Dixon, Mike Rafter and myself,
was the obvious one, as Tony Neary was still languishing in
the wilderness. The Midlands front row of Will Dickenson,
Peter Wheeler and Robin Cowling had given the All Blacks a
gruelling afternoon and, with Fran Cotton suffering from a
calf injury, it made common sense to pick those three as the
England unit. In the event, Wheeler and Cowling got the nod,
but Will Dickenson was left out; Barry Nelmes, a loose-head,
was brought in at tight-head.

The selectors' foolishness was further compounded when
John Scott, a second row forward they had just spent a season
grooming into a number eight, was moved forward to partner
Bill Beaumont. His move was not helped by the daunting
prospect of facing one of the best line-out jumpers in the
world, Andy Haden. England's two best middle-of-the-line
jumpers, Nigel Horton and Maurice Colclough, were ignored.
This badly chosen scrum was rightly seen by the New
Zealanders as the weakness they would exploit unmercifully
in the international; many agreed the selectors had already
dug our grave with their choices. I was pleased to see the
burly Tony Bond in for his first cap, but found it difficult to
understand the thinking behind some of the other selections.
Fran's absence had created a problem, but there was no
excuse or need to go into the match without a specialist
tight-head. If any single lesson should have been learnt from
the disasters of the seventies, it was that you have to pick
specialists in key positions; the folly of not doing so had cost us
dear on many occasions.

The proof of this came on the Saturday, when it was
obvious to everyone at Twickenham that we had played right
into the All Blacks' hands. Both New Zealand tries came from
English inadequacy at the line-out and the visitors were well

worth their 16 points to 6 victory. Neither my form, nor that of my Gosforth colleagues Peter Dixon and Malcolm Young, was anything to write home about; my hesitancy suggested I had been away for quite a while, or was I winning my first cap all over again?

Still, being back in the white jersey with the red rose was an amazing experience, especially as only a few months previously I was doubting my ability ever to play again at any level. But it is interesting to note how quickly priorities can change; from the initial delight at being back amongst the boys, my mood transformed to one of disappointment at losing and at the way we had lost. I set my mind thinking about how we could improve the set-up before the championship began. The selectors rightly came under a lot of criticism; Sandy was rather defensive for once and then attacked the system he was part of. 'Who can be more disappointed than us? We felt we had the core of the side we tried to build and we had injuries which eliminated players from key positions. When England are lambasted I would expect a fair amount of criticism and we have to accept it, but we have two months' breathing space and there are lessons to learn. You can't know it all. The game in England has to sort itself out at club and county level; I'm not trying to pass the buck – in terms of fitness we have quite a lot of ground to cover.' At least us northern players had a chance to redeem ourselves the following Saturday when the All Blacks visited Birkenhead Park. Eight of us had taken part in that Twickenham débâcle, but the North's preparation was far more organized than England's and we certainly went into the game with a lot more chance of winning. Two penalties from Malcolm Young gave us a 6–nil lead after half an hour. It was important we hung on to that lead to the interval. Graham Mourie's side had gained a reputation for striking back immediately and that is exactly what they did as a try and conversion from Brian McKechnie levelled the scores before Brian added a penalty to take his side 3 points in front. The score remained at 9–6 as we battled hard to try and emulate the North West's Warrington achievement. Our last chance went astray when Malcolm missed a late penalty and the New Zealanders just stayed ahead. The Neary/Uttley/Dixon back row was in harness that afternoon and a very enjoyable time we had. Peter and I, like the other England players, felt we had made up for our poor showing the previous week and had helped to restore some dented pride. Pride and confidence, though, were never far away in the north during the seventies and we never doubted our ability to turn it on for our country – when we were asked, that was.

My journey back to the big time continued when I scored a try for Northumberland in our victory over Notts, Lincs, & Derbys, which took us into the county championship final for the first time since 1936. That match, held in an almost deserted Twickenham on the last Saturday of the year, was a bitter disappointment. Middlesex didn't so much win the title as we threw it away, with one of our poorest displays for many a season. An injury in our scrum meant I spent the second half in the second row and several key players were well below their best.

That disappointment and England's poor display apart, the first few months of my comeback had given me far more than I had the right even to hope for. The New Year saw me recover my last link with the past when I was made captain of England in the senior side for the final trial on 20 January, when England were missing from the opening international Saturday of the season. Most of the mistakes from the New Zealand defeat had been recognised. Will Dickenson was at tight-head for England with John Scott moved back to number eight for the Rest fifteen. The Rest's second-row partnership of Maurice Colclough and Nigel Horton was up against Bill Beaumont and John Butler. The most pleasing aspect for most of us was the reinstatement of Tony Neary; his was a two-year exile that nobody outside the selectors could understand.

The trial was another weird afternoon; three periods of play were held, the first of forty minutes, and the other two of thirty. My personal involvement ended with a bruised thigh and so I missed the final session. John Butler moved back to number eight and Nigel Horton moved across to join Bill.

We were billeted at Bisham Abbey that night and would

have a run-out on the Sunday. When we returned there that Saturday night, our coach Peter Colston came up to me with a suggestion. He said that as we had the so-called top thirty players in the country all gathered together, this might be an ideal opportunity for us to discuss amongst ourselves what we thought was good and bad in the current set-up. The idea, I was led to believe, had originated from Sandy.

I told the lads that it had been recommended that we see how we felt about the national scene. Peter Wheeler brought up a matter about which we had all felt increasingly worried. This was the number of tracksuited selectors involving themselves in our squad sessions. This did highlight a problem which had got seriously out of hand. I remember the All Blacks captain Graham Mourie turning up at one of our training afternoons at St Mary's College at Twickenham; he could not believe that so much outside interference was tolerated by the players and coach. Graham could not imagine the late Jack Gleeson, the All Blacks coach at the time, allowing a selectors' cooperative. We appreciated the selectors' motives and never doubted their intentions for a moment, but a side has to be singleminded in its approach and attitude. We wanted to work alone with Peter Colston whose authority was being seriously undermined by all these intruders.

Other matters raised at our meeting was the way wives and girlfriends were treated and generally looked after during the international weekends. A call was also voiced for a more consistent approach from selectors, so that players could gain the confidence to express themselves naturally in internationals without fear of getting dropped for the slightest mistake. These were the main points from a meeting which was held at the instigation of the chairman of selectors, and in an orderly, friendly and good-humoured manner.

The team for the first international was announced a couple of days later and I was back as captain. Scotland were the opponents and this revived memories of my leadership debut only two years earlier. So much had happened since then, but I was very grateful to be back and to be given another chance of leading England to success. Poor Will Dickenson failed to make the team again; seldom has a player come so close to international honours without being capped. Instead, Gary Pearce, a newcomer with less than a year's senior rugby with Northampton behind him, was chosen. Nigel Horton and Tony Neary returned to the pack and Neil Bennett was back at fly-half after a four-year absence. Alastair Hignell returned at full-back in place of Dusty Hare and the side had the overall strength which had been lacking against the All Blacks.

Our schedule included a Sunday workout at St Mary's the week before the match. The day before Gosforth's cup game at Esher had given me much-needed match practice in a weekend when many games were cancelled because of the weather. The press were at our workout and noticed that the selectors were taking a back seat for once. Obviously, word had filtered back to the journalists that something had happened at Bisham the week before to make the selectors become more inconspicuous. I remember being collared by Barry Newcombe, David Frost and Tony Bodley in particular and asked; 'What's all this about a players' revolt?' I answered that we had been asked to get together and discuss our views on the rugby scene and the England set-up. We felt that there was too much outside interference and wanted to be allowed to get on with the job amongst ourselves with Peter Colston. Peter's trouble was that he was not forceful enough, but he was a good technician and we built up a good relationship during my two spells as captain. People on the training field who were not either players or the coach were not helping England's cause at all.

My brief response turned into an impromptu press conference on the side of the training pitch and my role was deemed to be one of revolutionary leader rather than captain. The next day's papers had me doing everything from 'barring the selectors from interfering with the squad session' to 'banashing selectors' to 'feeling strongly about the rights of player power'. Although none of these was the case, I did feel that players are the ones who are ultimately held responsible for what happens on the field and, as such, should have some sort of say in matters. The inference from the press was that now I was back in the driving seat things would be done

138

the Uttley way. In fact, though, I was only passing on the opinions which had been expressed by the squad as a whole – nothing more. I also added that England would never find success under the present structure and that leagues were necessary if we were to instil a competitive approach and make England a force again. What with these comments and the 'players' revolt', my name was plastered all over the Monday papers.

My intentions, like those of the selectors', were honourable, but this affair made them begin to wonder about the wisdom of this rebel returning as captain into the establishment fold. The captain of England's rugby side has a powerful position; rugby's growing attraction had made him a national personality. His views, whether the RFU liked it or not, had to be respected and were likely to be given plenty of space in the media. Personally, although my form was improving with every game, I had not yet felt anywhere near as physically fit as I had done before the injury. The absence of regular training was not helping and every eighty minutes of rugby left me absolutely exhausted. On the field I still wasn't contributing as much as I should have been and there was a long way to go yet. Having told the selectors, to 'Lay off', as the papers put it, I would have to watch myself from now on; I was getting the impression that the establishment displeasure was not so much at the fact that the England captain was making the wrong noises, but at the fact that he was daring to make any noises at all.

The build-up to the Scotland game was right, and reminiscent of that two years previously. I would have been delighted with a similar performance and result. Well, I got the performance, but not the result. The match ended in a frustrating 7 points to 7 draw, but the line-out tally of 27 to 6 and the rucks of 22 to 6 in our favour demonstrated our domination.

We could not have got off to a more perfect start. In the third minute, Nigel Horton leaped high to win good ball at the line-out in the Scottish twenty-two. The ball sped along the back line and, with Alastair Hignell timing his run into the line beautifully, the space was created for Mike Slemen to score in the corner. This was the classic try. Although Neil Bennett failed with the conversion, he added a penalty in the fifteenth minute to put us 7 points to nil in front. From that point we lost our way and that early promise didn't materialize. England's forward control counted for little as Malcolm and I played like we had never even met each other before. My annoyance was made worse when I had to leave the field ten minutes from the end after a bang on my thigh had deadened the nerves.

After the game, I wasn't that depressed with our showing; several times we were a pass or tackle away from scoring and, considering the display against New Zealand only two months earlier, this was a distinct improvement. Maybe I went over the top in defence of the side and came out with some naive comments – the press were not of a similar view. My public opinion was, 'I see this as a start of a new era. I just wish we could have ended up with the result our display deserved. I felt it was some of the best rugby we have played for a while and I was disappointed to see some reports in the Sunday papers which weren't too complimentary. I know we can go on to better things. It was amazing that we didn't get the victory we deserved. After recent performances I don't think we could have asked for a better display.'

According to the Monday press, I was now inhabiting the same cloud-cuckoo land as the selectors. They were probably right; we could have asked for a better display, but considering the annihilation of the pack against New Zealand, the improvement of the scrum was all we could have expected basically in such a short spell of time. At least we had found the platform for future success and the backs had had many chances to show their paces against the Scots; after such neglect, it was going to take them time to get used to handling the ball again. But I could understand the disappointment that afternoon as many people trailed out of Twickenham.

The selectors only made one change for the journey to Dublin. Sadly, the man to go was Malcolm Young, after ten consecutive games for England, the most since Dickie Jeeps had retired. My form had obviously had something to do with his demise, but, unlike Steve Smith after our defeat in

Wellington in 1973, Malcolm never held a personal grudge! I thought he was being made a token scapegoat, especially when the selectors brought back one of the forgotten men of England's 1975 tour of Australia, Peter Kingston. Trying to understand why they had left out an established and reliable player for one who, despite having been around for a long time, had never suggested that he could solve any of England's scrum-half problems was an impossible exercise.

Life on the road was hard and when an opportunity presented itself to change career paths yet again I gave it great thought. At the end of January, Terry had discussed the idea of opening a sports clinic in Hemel Hempstead to deal with sports injuries as well as to provide a scheme for keeping executive businessmen fit and healthy. The idea appealed because rugby was dominating my life again; each day, and night, just didn't provide enough hours to devote the energy I wanted to my family, job and rugby. Things could not carry on as they were, so I accepted Terry's offer and we set about establishing Forward Health.

These plans took a back seat as the Irish match approached. I was well aware that we needed a good result or the selectors would start disbanding the team. The weather was atrocious that Thursday morning as I had to make a 5.30 start from the house to be sure to get to Newcastle station in time for the early train to London. The snow was piled high and it took over an hour of careful driving to reach my destination. The scene at the station was like something out of *Doctor Zhivago*, with snow providing a thick camouflage everywhere and everbody buried under layers of clothes. Cups of tea from the crowded buffet were the only relief as we waited for the train, which was delayed for over an hour because of frozen points. The journey brought little comfort either, because the train lacked heating. Every year when the cold weather sets in, the railways are as ill-prepared as before to cope with it.

I wasn't the only one who was late for the training at the St Mary's Ground. Derek Morgan had given himself a hell of a fright when he'd turned round in his new Rover on the A40. Although we made a late start, the session went without any

141

hitches and there were no problems. I seemed to be feeling the cold more than usual, but I put this down to the freezing train journey.

By the time we had flown to Dublin the next morning, I was shivery and really feeling the worse for wear. When we landed, the coach took us straight to Lansdowne Road before going to the hotel for lunch. I skipped lunch and went straight to bed. By the evening, my temperature was a 105 degrees and Andy Ripley was sent for as cover just in case John Scott had to leave the replacements' bench and take my place. Andy always points to the chance of a quick call-up like this as being one of the benefits of living near Heathrow airport. Whatever bug I had, it was a quick worker; I had never been laid low so quickly and so effectively. Even if I felt better in the morning, there was no knowing how much the illness would have taken out of me. For in good health, I still wasn't feeling as strong as I'd like to be. After all I had been through, this was the final straw.

Saturday morning found me in much the same state and Sandy came along to see how I was doing. I said I was still ropey and didn't think I could make it. I thought that would be the final word, but he asked then if I wanted to play. Of course I wanted to play, he did not need to ask, but there was no way I could.

I felt at the time that he was implying that I was taking the easy way out and deserting my team. There was no way I would have been any use to them or to England in my condition and I felt a deep sense of resentment at such an insinuation. Coming over for a free weekend was not my style and Sandy, better than most people, should have known I would not try to free-load.

The doctor confirmed that I was one of the many sufferers of what was popularly called twenty-four hour flu – it would be gone in a day, but that wasn't any good for me or England. After all that hard work here I was out of the team again. The Irish coach Noel Murphy came in to see me and commiserated with my predicament.

So, instead of leading England onto the field, I was in the room of the president, Stanley Couchman, watching the action on television. There was no compensation there, as England reverted to their stuttering style and were beaten more decisively than the 12 points to 7 scoreline suggests. And the growing realization that the flu was disappearing as quickly as it had arrived did nothing to alleviate my feelings about the whole weekend. Another day's grace and I would have been okay.

By the evening I was fit enough to go to the banquet, though I wonder now whether it would have been better and more sensible to have adopted a low profile and just merged into the background. To all intents and purposes I looked perfectly well and this may have fuelled the arguments about whether I should have played or not.

Perrier water was my only refreshment during the dinner, but as the evening wore on, I felt much better physically and so more depressed at missing the game and the way the side had played. I decided to drown my sorrows and disappeared into the Dublin night with Terry Moule and Budge Rogers. Sunday morning confirmed the success of my suicide mission and I was able to reflect on the events of the weekend. I was still captain of England, officially, and the side had played badly without me. With me playing they might not had been any better, but I was trying to deal with facts. Yet, I had to admit that this latest Uttley withdrawal could lose me the captaincy for a second time – again without playing.

Out of Favour, But Not Alone!

The team wasn't announced until Thursday and because Sandy hadn't been in touch with me I did not think there would be any major changes. In fact, he had rung up on Wednesday, but I was on the road and he would not tell Kris anything. I had forgotten all about the team and just caught the end of a news bulletin on the car radio while driving home along the coast between Scarborough and Beverley. Those few words were nearly enough to cause me to swerve off the road. ' ... and Beaumont will captain the side.' Well, that wasn't entirely unexpected and at least I could concentrate on re-establishing myself as England's top number eight. Driving through Leamington I decided to pick up the *Evening Chronicle* just to see who else was in the team. I soon discovered who was not in the side – me! For the first time in my life I had been dropped; and without playing, too. What had I done to deserve this? The news was all the more shattering because I had discovered it like any other member of public, from a newspaper. I would have thought my position – or rather ex-position – as captain of my country would have entitled me to a little more consideration than that. Not only was I out of the side, but there was no room for me even amongst the replacements. No half measures by the selectors this time ... I was out on my ear.

I rang up Mickey Weston that night to find out what was happening. For once, he was evasive and embarrassed: 'I don't feel at liberty to say anything. You'd better get in touch with Sandy yourself.'

Before I could, I had the chance to read his comments in the papers; what a useful source of information they were

Above left: Bill Beaumont and I compete for a line-out ball in a Northumberland-Lancashire county game in 1975. Later we shared many triumphs together

Above right: One of the last photographs before I grew the moustache which has remained a permanent fixture. The textbook pass

Below left: What a day for Gosforth as they win the John Player Cup for the first time in 1976. Steve Gustard (with champagne) and cigar-smoking Harry Patrick celebrate in style joining Duncan Madsen in his bath

Below right: Another favourite photo — I don't know why, because I broke my leg a few minutes later in this club game against Richmond in 1976

The early months of 1977 were very good for me. After missing the 1976 John Player final, I was delighted to come back the following year and lead the club to triumph over Waterloo

That season had seen Malcolm Young join Peter Dixon and myself in the national team. Here, against Wales at Cardiff, Malcolm breaks, with Peter and me in support

Above left: The start of my troubles: being hauled up and down the Cheviots in a survival bag can't have helped my suspect back, however much I seem to be enjoying myself

Above right: Even training with the Lions in my Capital Radio sweatshirt I look okay, but that was the beginning and end of my Lions involvement on the 1977 tour

Below: I was initially given a couple of weeks' grace, but even being looked after by Kris and young Simon didn't ease my condition and I had to call off

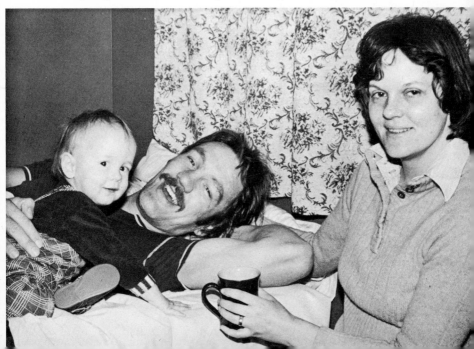

I was happy enough just to be back playing but I was overwhelmed not only to win back my England spot, but to regain the captaincy against Scotland. But the luck of the bounce did not run for us that day as Tony Neary and I found out

Opposite above: What a day it was for the North when, in November 1979, we hammered the All Blacks. Here Graham Mourie seems to have run into my arms

Opposite below: Chris Ralston and I may have been labelled the best-looking second-rows in the business, but only by ourselves

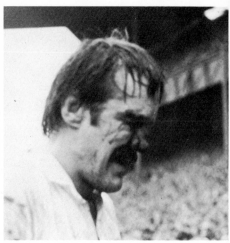

Above: It was obvious early on in the 1980 England-Wales clash that someone was going to be either sent off or taken off. In fact both happened. Paul Ringer is shown the way by referee David Burnett after quarter of an hour, and just before half-time I am led off with my face in a nasty mess

Below left: The Grand Slam back row of John Scott, Tony Neary and myself seen here taking on the French in Paris

Below right: In my new club colours (with a little help from Adidas) — the Geordie haven in the south: Wasps

Two former England captains, Fran and myself, give Bill Beaumont, the current captain, support in the Grand Slam triumph over Scotland

And here are the lads who clinched England's first Grand Slam for twenty-three years; (*back row*): Steve Mills (replacement), M. Bonnet (referee), Dusty Hare, Paul Dodge, me, Maurice Colclough, John Scott, Fran Cotton, Tony Neary, Mark Keyworth (replacement), Gordon Sergeant (replacement), M. Palmade (linesman); (*sitting*): Mr Thomas (linesman), Peter Wheeler, Clive Woodward, Mike Slemen, Bill Beaumont (captain), Steve Smith, John Carleton, Phil Blakeway; (*front row*): Alan Old (replacement), John Palmer (replacement), Ian Peck (replacement), John Horton

The current Uttley brood with Ben on Kris's knee and Simon on mine

turning out to be. Sandy said, and I quote, 'Roger has played very little rugby this year – about seventy minutes in the trial, the same period against Scotland and a cup game for Gosforth at Esher. In both the trial and the international he came off with a bruised thigh and this has restricted his training. We had to balance his qualities as captain against his potential to contribute to the full in what we expect to be an intensely physical game and we decided that his lack of fitness out-weighed his leadership.'

His comments were all the more ironic because one of the new caps in the side, centre Richard Cardus, was actually in hospital when the news of his selection came through – and the selectors did not even know. It was nothing serious and he was out soon after, but it emphasized how clued up they were. Also in for his first cap was Colin Smart, at the expense of Robin Cowling, and Andy Ripley retained his place on the replacements' bench. John Reason in the *Daily Telegraph* summed up my own feelings in his column: 'This is a curious decision because he [Roger Utley] is obviously just as fit now as when they chose him to captain England against Ireland last Saturday.'

Now I was out of the side, so that the famous Gosforth trio of Peter Dixon, Malcolm Young and myself had all been dropped by England in successive games. My absence did create something of a storm, not only in the north east. At best, the selectors were labelled 'inconsistent' – the less kind critics pointed to my supposed position as the instigator of the 'players' power' movement and they accused the establishment of conspiring to remove this rebel from the fold.

Sandy made contact later in the week and tried to explain that he had tried to get in touch before my demise became public news. I thought he might have tried harder than he did. Sandy merely reiterated the opinions he had made known to the papers and added that the selectors didn't feel that generally I was fit enough to take on the role. The earlier pronouncements of his selection committee made a mockery of that excuse, but I was not going to get involved in a slanging match on the phone about it. Public opinion seemed to be on my side but this sort of wrangling in mid-international season was neither doing English rugby any good nor was it likely to enhance the team's chances of further success that year.

As with Sandy on the phone, I did not want to become involved in a pointless public argument about my demotion. I had been dropped as England's captain and as England's number eight. I wasn't happy with the situation, but that was that. Outwardly I may have been angry, but inwardly I was hurt by what I felt was a betrayal and desperately sought the real reasons for my dismissal. Was it really to do with the 'players' revolt' after all? The RFU could sniff revolution if one of their members ordered a vodka and tonic instead of a traditional g and t; the committee resented players who became too big for their boots and would look for any excuse to do them down. Since all that press coverage, I had noticed a cooling off in their dealings with me. Also, my views about leagues and a competitive structure based on a club system was in direct opposition to the county-structured RFU; like any endangered species, they will lash out at anything which threatens their survival, which may not necessarily be the same as the game's.

Many, too, had disagreed with my comments following the Calcutta Cup match. 'A start of a new era' was not exactly how a lot of people had viewed the afternoon's proceedings, and they wondered how strong were the rose-coloured glasses I was wearing. Judging from the pitch is not always the best place; neither is watching in the stand.

There was some resentment, too, about Terry following in my trail, like a batman or latter-day Svengali. Most of these complaints reached my ears after I had been left out. However, anywhere he had come with me in the official party had been with the permission of the RFU. Terry had been part of the squad in Dublin, but only after being given the go-ahead by Colonel Morgan. Maybe some people thought I was receiving preferential treatment and did not like the thought of an outsider being involved in the official party. Terry wasn't everybody's cup of tea and wasn't someone who would sit meekly in the background and let his opinion go unvoiced. If, though, at any time the authorities had said that I was old enough to look after myself and didn't need a babysitter, then naturally I would have conformed to their wishes. When I had spoken to Mickey on the phone, I asked him if my association with Terry had anything to do with being left out and he assured me that it had not done me any harm.

Perhaps the simple truth was that I had come back too soon. I knew that I wasn't the player I was before my serious back trouble and that complete recovery would take a couple of years. Perhaps the selectors were thinking of the old Roger Uttley when they picked me first as number eight, then as captain, and not the new model who was still being run in.

The selectors had been very determined to bring me back quickly and they could not really blame me if I didn't match up to the exaggerated image they had of me. There could be no doubt that I was experiencing some exceptional highs and lows in my sporting life. The whole affair was making me rather paranoid and I realized that it would be better to dwell on other matters, especially as this time I saw no way back. Luckily, business life took over again and Forward Health was opened in March; the family moved down to Hemel Hempstead a month later. Leaving the north east after ten years was a great wrench, although my ties with that area will remain forever.

In the short term I kept up my playing connections with Gosforth until the end of the season. England won their following international against France by a single point. An exciting victory, yes, but little basis for the overwhelming optimism that prevailed as they travelled to Wales hoping to prove it was England's year at last. A win against Wales could have meant the championship, or at the very least a share of it. But England were crushed under the Welsh steamroller as the Principality notched up their fourth Triple Crown in a row. The 27 points to 3 defeat was England's heaviest defeat by Wales since 1903, when they went down 25 to nil. Five Welsh tries, including one by the veteran warhorse Mike Roberts, drowned all hope of an English revival.

Watching in grim satisfaction from the outside was no consolation; I saw everything we had built up since that New Zealand defeat well and truly thrown away. Neither was it any real consolation when looking back to see that with all the games I'd missed, I had never been on the end of a real hammering like that.

Gosforth were again going great guns in the John Player Cup and faced Moseley in the semi-final. Then for the first time ever we lost a national cup game at home as Moseley clinched a 6 points to 3 victory with a pushover try. For once the illustrious Gosforth back row got it all wrong and stood up too early, which allowed the Moseley scrum to plough their way over our line for the winning score.

Being out of the England side had taken me down a peg or two, but I had the ladder kicked from right under me when the squad to tour the Far East that summer was announced. England were under new mangement for this journey; Budge Rogers was the chairman of selectors and in charge of the touring party, Mike Davis, who had enjoyed great success with the England schoolboys, had taken over as coach. Both Tony Neary and Nigel Horton were unavailable, so I thought that as my experience, especially, would be of benefit to the youngsters, there was a good chance I would return to the fray. It was all a question of just how far 'out' I was, and only the selectors knew the answer to that. Suddenly everybody knew – my name was missing when the touring party was announced.

This was an even bigger setback than losing the captaincy and my number eight spot. The real insult wasn't so much being left out; the slight came from the quality of players they had chosen instead. Every touring party needs experience ... the 1975 tour of Australia had proved that in no uncertain manner. Still, there was no room for me or Peter Dixon, with Bob Mordell and Toby Allchurch joining Mike Rafter in the flank position. Tony Bond was also left out, as were two England scrum-halves of the season, Malcolm Young and Peter Kingston. Their replacements, Ian Peck and Chris Gifford, do not as yet feature in any international honours. John Horton was also left out, although at least the promise of Huw Davies was given a chance.

The selectors took five uncapped forwards with them to the Far East and the wisdom of their choices can be seen from the fact that two years later none of the five has made an international appearance. On his return, even Huw Davies was to languish out of favour for a season, before making a triumphant entry into the England side with the match-winning try against Scotland in 1981. I saw no way back from this ultimate snub and reckoned the selectors had dispensed with my services for ever.

The tour was an ideal opportunity to build for the future, but another chance was wasted. As in 1975, very few of the young players came back and made any sort of impression. You can't get boys to do a man's job; wisely, when the party returned, the selectors reverted back to experience before the 1980 campaign, having been pointed the way to success by the North's triumph at Otley. With the decade drawing to a close, the selectors were still experimenting and you only had to look back at the wreckage of many careers to wonder why. England's pack had been a respected unit in the seventies, and could have been turned into a really dominating force with a little more thought and consistency.

For me, the most-sinned-against man in English rugby during the seventies was a fly-half who appeared against me in my first senior game for Fylde. Alan Old was playing for Middlesbrough that day (he also turned out for Sheffield and Leicester). His meagre total of 16 caps was criminal when you consider how desperate England were for a controlling influence in the number ten jersey.

Initially, Alan struck me as arrogant and there was no reason to change that opinion when I got to know him better during the North East's challenge on the 1972 All Blacks; his words, though, were delivered in a typically forthright Yorkshire manner which was totally disarming. Alan was never afraid to express his views on the game – or any other subject for that matter. There was no searching for diplomatic words with him and I think he suffered frequent selectorial hardship because of his tongue. More important, Alan Old was a very good player. After being originally known by his initials, A.G.B., he was eventually christened E.N.T.Y. by Steve Smith. These initials stood for ears, nose and throat, referring to his large ears, his aquiline nose and great verbosity.

149

Somehow, he always appeared to be upset when referred to in this way.

Our friendship was cemented during the 1974 British Lions tour of South Africa. Phil Bennett may have ended up the king-pin of that test series, but in the early stages it was Alan Old who was in the driving seat. After scoring a record 37 points against the South West Districts, he was the victim of a tackle by the Proteas which was not so much late as posthumous.

That was the end of Alan's tour, but not of his consideration for the lads. Even with his leg in plaster, he tried to keep quiet when he went down with a severe bout of food poisoning on the morning of the second test, as he didn't want to disturb the lads' concentration. When J.P.R. and I discovered him, he was in a dreadful state and had been sick all over the place. I don't think I have seen anyone looking so ill in my life. With the help of Ken Kennedy, J.P.R. administered the correct medication and we cleaned him and the room up before putting him back in bed. He's never forgotten our kindness; I've never forgotten his sickness!

The selectors dallied with his affections over the next few years, but their neglect never seemed to affect his enthusiasm or dedication to the England cause; his presence was always a great boost for morale. Alas, even his indominable spirit was given a hell of a battering on the occasion of England's game against France in 1976. Alan was on the replacements' bench and, when first choice Martin Cooper failed a fitness test, everybody expected the natural progression of events to take place. But, in a turnabout which even for the England selectors was a *pièce de résistance*, Alan was kept where he was and Gloucester's Chris Williams leapfrogged from nowhere to play his only eighty minutes of international rugby. All this was too much for Alan, who eventually disappeared into the Paris night; even he was too upset for words. What a way to treat a senior player.

Oldie is a resilient soul and fought his way back. Paris, this time in 1978, was the scene of his final international appearance, when England were beaten as much by injuries to Peter Dixon and Andy Maxwell as by the French. After some of the previous surrenders in France, the 15 points 6 defeat was a reasonable showing considering the circumstances. Alan kicked two penalty goals, but found himself out of the side yet again for the next match. He kept going, though, and, the North's triumph at Otley provided for Alan – as it did for several of us – a more than adequate reward for not throwing the towel in. When he returned to the reserves bench for the 1980 championship, Alan contributed a lot to the Grand Slam side although he didn't play; his great belief in his own ability helped to spread confidence through the side.

One myth about him was that he was solely a kicker; Alan was a stylish fly-half who was very good with the ball in his hands.

Another who shared that Otley triumph, and also many of Alan's disappointments, was Peter Dixon. Apart from his mum, I am probably P.J.'s greatest fan. When I first met him, he had just returned from the 1971 Lions tour and was something of a celebrity in the region. Dave Robinson, who had been persuaded to join Gosforth from Birkenhead Park after the England tour to the Far East the same year, managed to entice Peter to the club soon after. One night in a pub Peter was christened 'Lenny' by Brian Patrick – something to do with him wearing his Lions blazer. He's been Lenny to the Patrick brothers ever since; initials are rather too subtle and sophisticated for them. Peter was the final addition to our back-row trio and we were to enjoy many happy years together.

Like Alan, Peter was rather outspoken and this may have contributed to his loss of the England captaincy in the early seventies. His manner was always charming, but his seemingly endless sojourns at academic establishments fashioned a rather casual manner and he could occasionally be unreliable. His classic was on the morning of the England fifteen's game against the USA at Twickenham, when he returned to the hotel after a walk only to be confronted by the chairman of the selectors, who wanted to know why he had missed the team meeting. These absentminded moments were not reserved for England. At Gosforth he was invariably the last person to arrive before a game. But Peter always arrived, eventually, and we came to adapt to that. On and off the field he was invaluable to me in his advice and play. Although my ball-channelling was not the greatest in the world and I would often take the wrong option, Peter and Dave, along with Malcolm, were there to help me out; we devised a style and system that was effective and great fun to play.

Peter is now on the RFU committee and no doubt telling the powers-that-be exactly how it is ... not how they'd like it to be. Peter was one of the outstanding British forwards of the seventies; Carwyn James recognized his enormous promise in New Zealand in 1971 when he played in three tests. But his talent was only tapped intermittently by England during the decade and they never used his immense talents to the full.

Wasted talent was not reserved to the north during this period. In the midlands there was Nigel Horton, who with Chris Ralston was England's top line-out jumper of the past ten years. Nigel was a rather surly and enigmatic character in his early days and there was an unpleasant side to his nature, which emerged most forcibly in that incident when he kicked Peter Dixon in the 1974 trial game. He was, however, a fine technician and was the sort of rugged forward needed to give England's pack bite. Nigel was never an easy person to get to know, but we developed a respect for each other over the years that eventually drifted into friendship. Even when he gave up his job as a policeman in the midlands and went to open a bar in Toulouse, he was more than willing to return home to press for an England place.

His uncompromising style made him a formidable opponent but like Alan Old he had been in and out of the England side since his debut in 1969. When he came in for Maurice Colclough before the 1980 game against Ireland, he became one of the very few international players whose careers spanned three decades. His joy turned to despair and his shoddy treatment that evening was a disgrace and is examined in detail in the next chapter. That episode marked the finish as far as he was concerned; how could he think otherwise?

David Rollitt, too, must have frequently wondered why he bothered. When he was brought back for the 1975 Calcutta Cup after a six-year absence from the international fray, his impressive form suggested he had been away far too long. This was confirmed on the subsequent tour of Australia when his play was one of the few saving graces on that disastrous visit. Yet when he returned home, it was back to the wilderness again. David was another who spoke his mind, and the selectors seemed to take that into account far more than his ability as a back-row forward.

These four were only the tip of the iceberg of a system which has kept many careers in cold storage over the decade. The players never understood what the selectors were trying to do; I'm not sure all the selectors did, either. A deep generation gap existed between the selectors and players. Rugby's new found status as a popular media sport as well as a target for sponsorship naturally brought increased pressures, some of which the old school was not even aware of. In addition, the attitude of the inconsistent selectors did little to instil confidence into the players on the field: one poor performance and you were out on your eye. Little wonder then that a safety-first attitude prevailed amongst the players, whose every step was marked with caution.

Thankfully, all these pressures and problems were behind me now. At least I had proved my point that I could return to stand the rigours of international rugby. Not many people would have given much chance of that at the beginning of the season. To be appointed captain of England again was a bonus, but circumstances dictated that my second reign only lasted one game, which gave me time to do very little or prove myself one way or the other. Being dropped without playing was a big blow and unfair, but there were others who had been treated much worse. And one of rugby's great attractions is that you are sometimes lucky enough to choose the level at which you want to leave the game. England might not want me, but there was always the club and county.

The summer was spent settling into our new house at Hemel and getting Forward Health moving. The only plans I had for the new season were to start off playing for a new club, Wasps, in north London. The northern connection was well known there in the form of Alan Blacks, a former Gosforth stalwart, and Tony Richards, the captain, who had served Fylde and Lancashire for many years and toured South Africa with England in 1972.

If I had still been on the road, my commitment to the playing side would have slowly wound down. But with a swimming pool opposite the Forward Health office, I was able to keep to almost daily sessions during the summer. With these, combined with regular training evenings, the strength that had been lost during my long lay-off was returning and I felt happier with my condition than at any time in my comeback season. There were occasional twinges from my back, but treatment, as much as I wanted, was on hand. With this newfound fitness, I also regained confidence in my own ability, which had been lacking for quite a while.

Now I was physically capable of taking people on and playing the type of game which had taken me to the top before. During the previous season, my existence had been one of survival; the better I now felt, the more I realized that this had been the case. Now I wasn't so much surprised that I had been kicked out of the side, rather that I'd been chosen in the first place after such a short spell back – they must have been keen! All this was leading up to the inevitable yet again: could I find my way back for a second time? My anger and hurt after the Irish game had subsided; those summer weeks allowed a more detached look at the situation and gradually I realized that English rugby and I still had a lot to give each other – selectors permitting.

London rugby turned out to be everything I'd been led to believe it was ... sociable, uncompetitive, soft and inconsistent. With the All Blacks arriving in October, I needed to make an immediate impact, so I returned north to play for Northumberland in the county championship. It wasn't an England place I was after, but a spot in the North fifteen which was to face the All Blacks at Otley a week before the international at Twickenham. With so many old friends being considered for the side, I sensed that I might regret not making an effort for this one. The North West Counties had toured South Africa at the end of the summer and had built up a tremendous team spirit which was to serve the North well.

154

That tour was the motivation behind Steve Smith's efforts to get slim and stay fit, with a little help from Fran Cotton. Both had played against the All Blacks at Warrington in 1972 and were keen to repeat that experience. With Peter Dixon still around, it was odds on that he would join Tony Neary and me in the back row, but he was unlikely to carry on much further after that.

There was no way that I was going to let the lads hold a party like that without seeking an invitation. The invite duly arrived. Our first training session under Des Seabrook was a revealing affair. The selectors could not believe their luck. This was the team they wanted to represent the north ... and immediately the feeling was right. The senior players all wanted to do well for each other; this was a crucial factor and obvious to everyone there. With Peter at number eight, I packed down on the flank. As in South Africa in 1974, I felt I might be putting myself at risk there but, again as in 1974, the quality of players around gave me a great confidence to do well.

In the pre-match chat, Mickey Weston said, 'We've picked a side to do the job and for some of you good performances might win England spots.' The national side was to be picked the following day at Leicester before the squad session.

Then Des Seabrook got up and said, 'These buggers,' meaning the England selectors, and he looked at Mickey 'have made their minds up already. They're convinced that the North aren't going to be able to produce the goods. That's an insult to all of you and you know there's only one way to prove the point. Go out and destroy them!'

Mickey was visibly wincing under Des's accusations, but we all knew that the coach was speaking the truth. The selectors had even tried to get Steve Smith pushed out of the side for Nigel Melville, the recent England Schools scrum-half, so that a good display would give the selectors the chance to bring him into the England team for the international. We knew it would take an almighty performance from us to make them change their minds. Today, our loyalties lay with the other players in the side and with the north.

The atmosphere in the dressing room was very relaxed,

155

which was strange for a game of this stature. We were facing the All Blacks test side and they had convincingly beaten the Scots at Murrayfield the Saturday before. But in face of such a daunting task, we were totally calm; we knew for a fact that we were going to go out there and beat them. Nobody had any worries about the ordeal; we just wanted to go out and get amongst them.

Dressed in British Lions red with a white rose badge and The North spelt out underneath, we charged out. The pitch was encased by a mass of cheering spectators, some of them swaying in the trees at the far end. Like us, they knew that today was going to be something special.

The lesser names in the pack – by that I mean those players who hadn't captained England, unlike Bill Beaumont, Fran Cotton, Tony Neary, Peter Dixon and myself – were magnificent. Colin White was a veteran campaigner, having come close to an England cap on several occasions. There were some worries expressed beforehand about the throwing-in of hooker Andy Simpson, but he came good on the day (he has since gone from strength to strength and sat on the England bench throughout the 1981 campaign). Jim Sydall, partnering Bill in the second row, had an impressive day in the line-out and was in no way overawed by the presence of Andy Haden. Behind the scrum, Steve Smith and Alan Old with their usual calming influence kept a tight control. Even when the All Blacks did win balls their back line could use, Tony Bond was in devastating crash-tackling form in the centre and created all sorts of havoc in the visitors' midfield. Beside him was Tony Wright, a late entrant to senior rugby, who showed a rare poise even in these tough conditions. ·

John Carleton's youthful promise just edged out Peter Squires's experience for the right wing spot; Peter's cause had not been helped by the Yorkshire selectors shunting him around in their back line. Mike Slemen, on the other wing, was a world-class footballer, equally good in defence as in attack. The only foreigner in our midst was the full-back, Kevin O'Brien, who was to appear for Ireland later that season and who had been in phenomenal goal-kicking form for Lancashire in the preceding weeks. He was not required in that capacity at Otley, because Alan Old was in attendance. That afternoon, anyway, penalty goals were not important as we inflicted the most humiliating defeat a touring All Blacks side has ever suffered in the United Kingdom outside international matches.

The All Blacks were taken apart, piece by piece. We were only seven points in front at the interval, but the All Blacks had had the benefit of a fierce wind. With Alan Old in charge at fly-half, whatever happened now we would be able to keep them at bay. But the mood was still attack; two tries by Tony Bond, who was thoroughly enjoying himself in such a physical arena, gave us a 17 points to 3 advantage after an hour.

Our confidence was so complete that we kept on the attack. New Zealand managed to reduce the deficit when Stu Wilson scored a fine individual try. The last minutes belonged to the North, though, and produced the highlight of the game as far as I was concerned. Attacking down the left flank, we bundled the All Blacks off the ball; eventually Alan Old gathered before bobbing and weaving his way through to the line for our fourth and final try. Considering all the kicks in the teeth he had to put up with over the years, he richly deserved that moment. He missed the conversion, but no matter because the North had reduced the All Blacks threat to a rubble in the course of a 21 points to 9 thrashing.

Four tries was an amazing tally; New Zealand had only conceded a total of five tries on their 18-match tour of Britain the previous year. The thrilling, heroic victories of the North West and Llanelli in 1972 and of Munster in 1978 were emotional one-offs. This success was different. The All Blacks had been beaten at their own game and had been hounded off the park like never before in a provincial game. We hadn't even given them the chance to play badly. Many people claimed that this was the greatest performance by an English side outside the international team – and who was I to disagree? The cold-bloodedness of our triumph was calculated to precise detail. The 'famous five' England captains were as delighted as the rest, especially in view of Des's pre-match comments. Had we shown England the way? Well, we dug the road ourselves, tarred the surface and put up the directions.

157

With the All Blacks on the run, England had only to follow the North's example in a week's time and New Zealand would suffer a rare double defeat.

The evening took a sad turn when Peter Dixon told me that he had decided to call it a day and this was his final representative match. Hearing such news from your contemporaries is always a shock, and Peter and I had built up a special relationship over the years. It was sad to think that never again would we take the field together. But what a way to go out! Peter had purposely hung on for this match and his judgement, as ever, had proved sound. I had thought after our performance that he might stand a chance of getting back in the England team, but Peter is not such a romantic and said that he had had enough of being mucked around. We did agree that it was one hell of a way to say goodbye.

During the evening many views were expressed about the composition of the England team for the international. There was no way that the selectors could ignore our performance, either as individuals or as a unit. How many of us would they choose? Kevin's Irish connections excluded him at full-back, where Alastair Hignell or Dusty Hare were likely to get the nod. There seemed no reason to upset the rest of the back line. Tony Wright had shown real class and John Carleton was likely to continue his rise to the top. All the rest were international players and, while Alan Old might not be in the current England squad, his experience and guile were necessary if the national team was to exercise the same control as we had shown. Well, that was six out of seven in the backs.

What about the forwards? With Peter unavailable, John Scott would play number eight and join Tony and I in the back row. Neither Maurice Colclough nor Peter Wheeler could be left out, and it was also expected that Colin Smart would be the loose-head. Four out of eight in the scrum, but ten North players in all. These changes would only strengthen the team and, with the 'Otley Blueprint', England could not fail to give the All Blacks another hammering.

These discussions may have taken place in the euphoric haze of Otley, but I have no reason to doubt the logic of such a selection, even today. Individual aspirations were not the priority at Otley, but I was more than satisfied with my own form. The new, improved Roger Uttley was at last functioning as well as the old one and I was twice the player I had been the previous season. Now I was back at my best and looking forward to fulfilling a memorable double triumph over the All Blacks.

The celebrations were curbed that night because we had to gather at Leicester the following morning; many of us considered that our task was only half complete. In Leicester, the mood was blatantly optimistic as we gathered in the big room to hear Budge Rogers announce the team, starting with the full-back spot.

'Full-back, Hare.' Fair enough: Alastair Hignell was suffering from injury problems.

'Wings, Carleton and Slemen; centres, Bond and Preston.'

Tony Wright hadn't made it.

'Fly-half, Cusworth; scrum-half, Smith.'

Talented though Les Cusworth was, he hadn't been capped before nor had he ever played with Steve – yet another experiment.

'Front row, Smart, Wheeler, Cotton.'

As expected.

'Second row, Beaumont, captain, Colclough.'

As expected.

'Back row, Neary, Scott and ... Rafter.'

Rafter! I just couldn't believe it. Steve Smith said my mouth gaped open and my jaw just about hit the floor, such was the look of amazement on my face. They HAD chosen the team before the North game; there could be no other reason for ignoring the evidence of their own eyes!

II

Back to Ringer, Wheel and the Championship

That team roll call was one of the worst moments of my life. After all I had been through, the many heartaches, this was the bitterest pill. After the North's victory, I felt like a three-times winner; now I was a three-times loser. A place on the replacements' bench meant that I hadn't been totally ignored, but there was little consolation in wearing the number twenty-one shirt. I should have known better than to assume that I would definitely be in the side, especially after all that had gone before ... but I had thought the lessons of Otley were obvious to one and all. Now I knew what Peter Dixon meant about not wanting to be mucked about any more. The session that followed was not exactly pleasant; I had to take on the role of cannon-fodder as the selected side went through its movements.

The delight of Saturday had become the dismay of Sunday as I travelled back home. I didn't think I was wrong to be so upset, but maybe I was taking it too personally and was treating this affair out of proportion. But Monday's papers confirmed my view: the selectors were given a roasting for not taking notice of the North's triumph. The comments of Budge Rogers, especially, showed he had not grasped what he had seen on Saturday. As well as not wanting to be 'over influenced' by one match, he added, on the topic of the North's seven representatives in the international team, 'I'm glad it's not more. It's asking a great deal of our players to raise their game to that peak so soon.' And what a frightening attitude from someone who hopes to manage the 1983 Lions to New Zealand. He'll have a lot of trouble picking his Saturday side in that case. Budge had just watched one of the greatest

160

performances from an English side ever, any side. Emotional, yes; but also cold, calculating and deliberate in its execution of a style which had destroyed the most-feared national rugby side in the world.

Otley had provided him with a dress rehearsal for the performance England needed, but now the show's director had changed several leading members of the cast because he was worried that they might not be all right on the night. The only explanation for such a change could be youth and inexperience ... but the players involved were veterans of Lions tours and many internationals, with the respect of everyone around. Even more important, players like Alan Old and myself had not only defeated the All Blacks at Otley, but we had beaten New Zealand on their own territory and were in no way in awe of the silver fern.

The pairing of Les Cusworth and Steve Smith might have been made in heaven as far as the selection committee was concerned, but it looked more like cloud-cuckoo-land to me. It certainly wasn't made on earth – the two had never played together before. They became another sad statistic: England's sixteenth half-back partnership in twenty-seven games. Les had matured a lot under the influence of coach Chalky White at Leicester, but he was not the sort of tactical kicker who could control and dominate the match as England needed.

Des Seabrook was as diplomatic in his comments about the team as he had been in his pre-match talk, but his feelings were generally those of rugby folk in the North and elsewhere: 'The selectors don't seem to have accepted what we have achieved. I was expecting nine or ten of the side to get to Twickenham. Instead there are only seven. How can they really explain leaving Roger out after his performance at Otley? There was nothing more a player could do – he was simply tremendous, like the rest of our back row.'

The All Blacks must have been delighted; we had played right into their hands. Nobody expected them to take their humiliation quietly and they would probably come out at Twickenham with steam belching from their ears; seeing most of the North lined up against them again, though, would have been a big psychological blow.

Watching from the bench was not a pleasant way to spend an afternoon, especially with England fumbling around like a bunch of novices. England were not capable of withstanding the inevitable All Blacks pressure or of controlling play as the North had done. New Zealand led by 10 points to 3 at the interval; then Dusty added two more penalties to reduce the deficit to one point. That was how it remained. A defeat which meant the promise of Otley had disappeared in a stroke: not through any fault of the players, but because the selectors – as they had done through the seventies – had failed to realize the strength of the regions and to use this to England's advantage.

It was so predictable, and depressing, that their folly would end in defeat; the long-suffering supporters were left wondering when all this madness would end. The great sadness of the whole affair was that there was no need for it. We had beaten the All Blacks out of sight the week before and there was no way, if the selectors had picked the right people, that England would have gone onto that park and lost. All they had to do was strengthen the North team with the best players from the rest of the country. Annoyingly, the team was not far from being an effective unit, but as on so many occasions crucial weaknesses affected the confidence and efficiency of the national side.

Strangely, after this comedy of errors, Kris and I had our most pleasant after-match evening. For her part, travelling down from Hemel made life a lot easier; by not playing, I myself was relaxed and fresh, enjoying the rituals of the international evening far more than I had done as a player.

Many people came up and said things would have been different if I'd been playing. Well, the game was past now, but I felt hopeful that I might come back for the championship. This latest All Blacks' defeat meant that the selectors had to examine seriously their policy. If England had won that day – and they might have just sneaked it – then England wouldn't have done so well in the championship. Losing that day forced the selectors, at last, to learn the lessons of form and experience.

The final trial was something of a farce. With so many call-offs and injuries, there was little to learn from the

proceedings. In fact, though, the final piece of our championship jigsaw was discovered, and a very vital one it was, too.
Before the trial, Saracens prop Clint McGregor was being
hailed as the great white hope. But when the team to play
Ireland was announced, he had been overhauled by Gloucester's Phil Blakeway, one of the most solid scrummagers I've
ever come across. In other areas, the selectors reverted to
experience, with John Horton back at fly-half, Alan Old
joining the replacements and me packing down with John
Scott and Tony Neary in the back row.

Everyone involved in the Otley victory knew the national
side could be just as successful. There was something there to
build on. We were all playing to a pattern and had the
experience and ability to impress that pattern on the opposition. The big question was whether we would be given the
chance to prove that in an England jersey. The selectors, after
a false start, said yes.

Their discovery of Phil Blakeway at this late stage was a
tremendous bonus: you couldn't budge him as far as scrummaging went, which was important for the back row because I
could now come off without affecting our push. Tony and I
were playing left and right, so there were times when I
worried that I might be suspect on the blind side. With a
secure scrum, I could take one step back and one step to the
side just to let the opposition scrum-half know I was there. If
the opposition won the ball, then it would be unlikely, with a
man standing there, that they would try an attack down the
blind; we had that area covered. John Scott and Steve Smith
would know what was going on, but Phil was the key. The
scrum would not move or wheel; his first duty was to
scrummage. This he could do even when not fully fit ... as
was to happen later in the season.

That completed our pack. With the object of the exercise to
go for control, Tony and I took John Scott to one side and
drilled into him that he was going to have to discipline himself
and play it tight, not going for walkabout as he had done
against New Zealand. John was a talented forward who had
been allowed too much of a free rein in some of his early games
for England. With Tony supplying the pace and good looks

and John and I adding the bulk and hulk, our back row was well equipped for all eventualities and emergencies.

In Bill Beaumont and Maurice Colclough pairing in the second row, we had the best duo in the British Isles (as they were to prove in South Africa later that summer). It had taken Bill a fair time to come to grips with the captaincy, but he was now in control, and the responsibility was no longer affecting his game. Maurice was one of the few who had benefited from the Far East tour: he had re-established himself as one of the most exciting young forwards in the world. And Phil could not join any better members of the front-row union than Peter Wheeler and Fran Cotton, both of whom had had enough of the bad old days and were looking to finish on a high note. Usually, the forwards had not been the root of England's problems in the seventies.

Steve Smith was now playing like the scrum-half his ability had suggested he would become after his introduction to the international scene in 1973. After missing the victory over New Zealand that summer, his form became rather haphazard as he drifted into a kind of never-never land. The North West Counties tour of South Africa was the beginning of his revival and Fran Cotton saw to it that his good work did not go to waste for once ... this was going to be his final chance. The Fran and Smithie double act continued off the field, Fran proving the perfect foil for Steve's special brand of humour.

Les Cusworth, like many fly-halves before him, was thrown onto the reject pile after the shortest of careers. John Horton returned. An oustanding schoolboy player, John had waited a long time for his big chance. But he had been dropped after the 1978 New Zealand defeat and then Neil Bennett and Les had filled the fly-half spot. At one time, after the Far East tour, it had looked as if Huw Davies might make a quick rise to stardom, but he fell badly out of favour on his return and was put in cold storage for a season. Steve and John knew each other well and were happy playing together, with John providing the kicking control that was missing against New Zealand.

Tony Bond and Nick Preston were compatible in the centre:

Tony was the hard man, with Nick providing the pace and a bit of flair. Mike Slemen's experience on one wing was balanced by John Carleton's raw running on the other and both were extremely dangerous in their own way. Dusty, while not the world's greatest running full-back, was very sound and one of the best goal-kickers in international rugby.

Everybody in the side felt the team was right – the balance was correct. Importantly, too, Mike Davis was settling in well after initial apprehension between him and the players. At first I had found him distant and rather dictatorial in his methods. In recent years I had become used to being consulted by coaches like Peter Colston and Des Seabrook as one of the senior professionals. Mike very quickly conveyed a feeling of 'them and us'. One of the problems was that the bad selection for the Far East tour meant that when he came to dealing with the squad for the New Zealand game, there were many new faces to contend with. These weren't young newcomers, but players like myself, Steve Smith, Fran Cotton, Tony Neary, John Horton and Tony Bond, all of whom were used to working with someone like Des Seabrook; up North it wasn't exactly a power-sharing system, but a think-tank was definitely in operation.

One of Mike's first directives at Leicester was; 'And now we are going to play one of my silly games.' I wondered whether he thought he was back with England Schools again. I hadn't been spoken to like that for a long time. Things were done very much his way that day. There is a story that after one of the internationals he was asked to go down and sing for the ladies who were having dinner. There was laughter all round when the news came back that he had confirmed our suggestions that his vocal choice had been 'My Way'.

I got the feeling that we were not being consulted and my mind went back to the comments I had made during my second spell as captain a year earlier: 'It's players on the field who ultimately carry the can. The selectors make the decisions and it's up to the players to get on with it. Ultimately, they are responsible on the day.'

Mike kept himself very much to himself at Leicester, apart from odd chats with Bill. I didn't think that that was the right way to get the best out of people. So, when I saw him alone having breakfast on the morning of the New Zealand game, I decided to tell him what I thought. These comments were not meant as a personal criticism of him in any way. When I said that I didn't think he was approaching this in the right way, he replied that he would be grateful for any help I could give.

'We senior players like to be consulted and we'd prefer if we decided together how we are going to play the game, rather than being told we are to do things this way and that. Even as a replacement, I'm concerned about the game and how we are going to play it as much as you are. I think it's important that we get a dialogue going.'

My respect for him increased immediately as it became obvious that he could take constructive criticism when he thanked me for coming to talk to him. His attitude did change and the assault on the championship truly became a team effort. But he still had one or two schoolmasterish tricks up his sleeve. For the team meeting later that morning we walked into a room at the Petersham Hotel and there was Mike, complete with overhead projector and key words on the different aspects of the game written down. Coming into the side as a newcomer, this might look impressive; Tony and I, though, looked at each other cautiously.

Another of Mike's initial problems was that he had been away from the senior scene for quite a few years and his experience of coaching had been restricted to looking after the England Schools side in the first half of the seventies. Mike had been very successful, but would he be able to deal with the big boys in the same way? Well, here we were back in the classroom again. I found the team-talk rather corny and it was obvious that Mike was nervous himself. He finished with 'Hope you've got it right,' and left with the other selectors trailing out after him ... rather like assembly at school. I was surprised that we weren't asked to stand as they left.

He persisted in his style and by the Scottish game both sides had compromised. Mike knew that we thought it had all been a bit of a joke; as he mellowed in his attitude, we began to appreciate the logic of his talks, which almost became discussions. Slowly through the season we identified with each other and with England's cause. His achievements, considering how long he had been away, were remarkable in that first season; he showed a refreshing willingness to learn from his mistakes and face problems head on. Some of my early hostility may have had its roots in my dissatisfaction with that New Zealand selection, for which he could hardly be blamed.

All the disappointments were put behind us as we waited the arrival of the Irish. After a magnificent tour of Australia the previous summer, Ireland were not only favourites to beat us, but stood a good chance – according to popular opinion – of winning the championship. They had won both tests in Australia, and what was even more remarkable, they did it after dispensing with the services of Tony Ward, who had scored a record 38 points in the 1978 campaign.

He had been hailed as Ireland's new saviour, but a young man by the name of Ollie Campbell was to appear on the scene and steal the glory in Australia. After returning from that tour, Tony flew to London to accept the Rugby World Player of the Year Award at the Painters Hall. I think he felt slightly embarrassed to be receiving this at a time when he could not get into his national side. Such are the ups and downs of rugby and sitting next to him at the luncheon I was able to explain, with easy reference to my own career, just how situations can change. His exile continued, though, and he was missing from the Irish line-up that faced us at Twickenham.

With Ireland's current form and our recent record, the men in green were hot favourites. That suited us just fine. There was a quiet but determined mood in the side as England took the field for the 1980 international championship. Our plan was to dominate up front, because that was where our strength lay. By using the principles of the North's win over the All Blacks, we were going to get amongst them, apply as much pressure as possible and get as many points on the board as possible.

We established that forward domination, but found ourselves 3 points to 9 down after 20 minutes, with Ollie Campbell in great kicking form. The pattern was familiar; surely we weren't on that same old road to ruin again. Our equalizing score came when, after pressing near their line, we tied up the Irish defence and Steve Smith had the simplest of tasks – to pick the ball up and dive over. Steve was also the instigator of the try that took us in front just before the interval. With his way ahead blocked, Steve kicked through to the Irish corner. Kevin O'Brien, their full-back, tried to kick the ball clear on the full; but he made a dreadful mess and Mike Slemen was on hand to gather and go over in the corner. It was the same Kevin O'Brien who had played at Otley, but he was being showed little consideration by his Lancashire colleagues.

Dusty duly converted both these tries and we turned round 15 points to 9 in front. With our control so complete, Ireland never had a look in during the second half. Dusty kicked his second penalty before John Scott picked up from a scrum and ran fifteen yards for a try, which he acknowledged by holding the ball aloft in one armed salute. The gesture did not reflect the mood of the side, which was uncompromising and undemonstrative; we didn't want to appear arrogant and the action was a personal one that the rest of the side felt did not suit the occasion. The only setback we suffered that day was when Tony Bond broke his leg after an hour and was replaced by Clive Woodward making his debut. Everyone was delighted with the result, 24 to 9 – as many points as the side had scored in the whole of the previous championship – and with our performance. We won so much good ball and kept such a tight control that we destroyed a side which had been highly rated. When you consider the way that they were to thrash the Welsh at the end of the season, it made a nonsense of their display against us. They were better than that, but they were not allowed to be. That's how we played it that season – with control – not allowing the opposition to play the rugby they wanted. Alas, like the night of our win over Scotland four years previously, the evening was spoilt by an action of such thoughtlessness it was incredible even by the standards of the England selectors. Nigel Horton had come into the side when injury forced out Maurice Colclough. Now living in France, the Midlands lock put in another solid performance and fitted in so well that our effectiveness was not reduced in any way. With a long way still to go, he would be useful to have around.

We all guessed that Maurice might regain his place, but tomorrow was another day.

Then after the dinner was finished and we were getting ready for the dance, I came across a very distressed Kay Horton. I inquired what was the trouble and she said that Nigel had just been told he wasn't playing in the next game. 'You're joking,' I exclaimed. It was obvious she was not. I went to find Nigel and asked him what had happened. He was in a terrible state: totally distraught and actually crying. He said that this was the finish as far as he was concerned: he didn't want to know any more.

Fancy telling anybody that his services wouldn't be required the night after he had played his guts out for his country! Budge was very lucky not to get planted by Nigel, who must have known in his own heart in any case that Maurice was likely to come back. Anything, though, can happen with injuries and loss of form and you would think the selectors would want to keep as many options open as possible. It was distressing to watch his humiliation – nobody deserved to be treated like this. I almost went to see Mike Davis myself, but told Bill instead, as I felt it was his responsibility. Bill came back with the excuse that it was a mistake ... but it had been done now.

A lot of the young players didn't appreciate what was going on, but the senior lads were disappointed with what had happened – England's magnificent man-management again! It was as if they were trying to think of the best ways to destroy that tremendous team spirit we had created that afternoon. The whole affair cast a gloomy shadow over the celebrations that was all the more devastating because the distress was totally unnecessary.

Maurice did come back for our game in Paris and was the only change from the side that had finished the game against Ireland. Poor Tony Bond would be out for the season and Clive retained his place.

Paris was certainly not a happy hunting ground for England; they had last won there in 1964 and had never been victorious at the Parc des Princes. Training in the damp in Paris and then Versailles we gained even more confidence because this weather was ideal for us. Instead of sharing with Tony, I was stuck with John Scott – from beauty to the beast, you may say.

As a precaution with my back, I slept with the mattress on the floor to give a more solid base. But my nightmare of further back trouble became a reality when I awoke in the morning to find that my back, after two days' training and travelling, had seized up again. Oh no, here we go again. John Scott was oblivious to the world as I dragged myself off the floor. It was about half-past six and there was no one about. It had always been my big fear that I would have to cry off on the morning of a big game like this . . . I knew all the problems it would create.

I needed to get heat on my back so I went into the shower; there I was hobbling around in there, like Corporal Jones from 'Dad's Army', thinking Don't panic, don't panic. I leant on the wall with one arm so that the hot water sprayed on the affected area, and eventually, after about half an hour, the situation began to ease. I felt fit enough to move around so I went to see Don Gatherer, being careful not to tap too loudly on his door because Doctor Leo was next door. Don opened the door rather bleary-eyed, but soon had his magic fingers working their miracles and I became one of the England team again.

The journey to the ground by motorcade was as exciting as ever and Steve Smith and I sat at the front enjoying the view of the four gendarmes on motorbikes carving out a path for us. If any cars are too slow to get out of the way, then the French police are not frightened to deposit a large boot into the sidepanel of the offending vehicles. This got us in the right mood for the battle ahead. By the time we had our photograph taken, the rain had stopped, but it was still overcast. The going was heavy, which suited our strong pack perfectly.

As you leave the changing room, you can get a view of the proceedings through the large glass doors. As we came out for the last time, the sun was streaming through the glass and I turned to Tony and said, 'Bloody hell!' The French with the sun on their backs are a dangerous lot; the warm atmosphere seems to fill them all with that traditional flair and daring.

170

Just to prove their point, their captain Jean-Pierre Rives, rounded off a thrilling movement to score a try in the opening minute. Seconds later we were back at the halfway line as though the game was about to start all over again; unfortunately, we were four points adrift and had plenty to make up.

That was just the sort of opening that had heralded several humiliating English defeats at French hands in recent years. To be behind our own line without having even broken into a sweat was a demoralizing feeling. Yet we were determined that this was not the beginning of another French avalanche. We'd been behind against the Irish and worked our way back; although we had made it difficult for ourselves, this was what we had to do again. And, with our pack in outstanding form, we slowly hauled ourselves back.

John Carleton and Nick Preston could not have timed their first tries for England any better and John Horton dropped goals either side of the interval to take England in front by 17 points to 7. I missed both these kicks because I was off the field receiving treatment. Joinel had tapped me behind the ear with his boot and I once again left the field with blood streaming down. In the medical room Mike was getting very agitated for the officials were asking irrelevant questions like the address of my doctor back home. I don't know whether this useless information was supposed to delay my return to the action, but luckily Doctor Leo came in and stitched me up. He said that Joinel's kick had just missed the cerebral artery – I was very lucky as the injury could have been quite serious.

All I wanted to do was to get back and I was delighted to find that our lead had increased from a slender 10 points to 7 into 17 to 7, courtesy of John Horton. That the side had raised their game because they were one short demonstrated why the 1980 side was different. Our scrum had been giving the French a terrible pasting, but as the game went on, and Phil Blakeway suffered from a rib injury, their forwards at last responded to the cheers of the French supporters. We faced a torrid time in the final minutes. When the French cut loose, then you're in big trouble ... and we played right into their hands by missing touch several times and allowing them back into the action. From one of those breaks, Averous went over.

Our plight was not helped when Caussade converted from the touch-line. But, after a traumatic finale, we just stayed ahead to register England's first win in Paris for 16 years.

The French had fought us every inch of the way and the game had been played at a tremendous pace; we all slumped exhausted in the dressing room, but the euphoria of winning made up for any physical tiredness. The only thing that annoyed us was that we had had the French on the rack and allowed them back into the game. We could sort that out later...

Evenings in Paris are always memorable, especially if you've also enjoyed the rare taste of victory. The dinner disintegrated into chaos when, after we had been presented with after-shave and records, John Scott, I think it was, discovered the records made impressive frisbees. If you didn't have your head knocked off by one of them, then a soaking in after-shave would follow. The French police are great, very protective, and they stay with you and enjoy the fun most of the evening. I went to bed reasonably early because of my headache, but the action continued well into the night. Clive Woodward had a beautiful velvet jacket destroyed and the following morning Steve Smith had more trouble with re-entry than any of the Apollo spaceships.

That victory rather unexpectedly had opened up all sorts of opportunities, not least the chance of the Grand Slam. At present we led the table with two wins out of two, Ireland, Scotland and France all having lost at least once. Our next game, against the only other unbeaten side – Wales – was the crunch and would decide whether this England team was different after all or just another side full of false promises.

As the importance of this game dawned on us, it soon became blatantly obvious to the media, who proceeded to give the confrontation an importance and significance which a rugby game simply does not merit. After all this exaggerated build-up, it was no surprise to anyone when the rugby bubble burst, or rather exploded, to disgrace everybody playing and more than a few others off the field that afternoon at Twickenham.

Labelled the 'match of the decade' which wasn't difficult as

172

we were only six weeks into the eighties – the ingredients for this battle came from a variety of sources. Six years had passed since England had last beaten Wales; even then the Welsh had complained about some 'blind Irish referee', and had refused to allow us even the smallest crumb of success. But Wales were on the decline; this was obvious to everybody. However low the Welsh fall, though, the one thing their supporters refuse to contemplate is losing to England. Now questions were being raised about whether their team would have the ability to cope with an England side with two wins under their belt. The English rugby press, so used to national disasters, had begun to build us up as the greatest thing since sliced bread and kept enthusing over our qualities.

Everything that could be thrown in the melting pot was. The papers alleged that Fran had called Graham Price a cheat for always taking the scrum down, and was going to sort him out. John Scott, too, was playing against three of his Cardiff colleagues and was going to take them on. You could not pick up a paper without some new revelation about the England – Wales contest.

Everybody was making something out of the match, which we as international players accepted as the norm. The man of the moment was Paul Ringer of Wales. It is his name that will live longest in the memories of this match, but even before he took the field, he was earmarked as the man most likely to . . . cause trouble. His performance against France a month earlier had later been analysed by television commentators: while he may have fooled the referee that day, his crimes could not get by the slow-motion camera and many felt that he should not have been chosen. What Paul Ringer felt about all this press coverage, I don't know, but that afternoon at Twickenham he played like a man who believed totally in his own publicity.

Inevitably, all the press baiting found its way into the minds of the players; it was impossible not to let the pressure get to you. Any confrontation was bound to lead to a duel because we were not prepared to bow to Welsh intimidation as England teams had done in the past; we would not accept that at any level. This was agreed before the game and because of the character that had developed in the side everybody decided to meet fire with fire. Now we were physically prepared to commit ourselves the way the Welsh do: totally and without consideration of life and limb – their's or their opponents. We had had enough of accepting second-best; this was our last chance – if we blew it now then there would be nothing left. That was the background to a game of rugby which was buried under more bad publicity than any other, before or since.

By the day of the match, you could cut the atmosphere with a knife; a terrible environment for a game of rugby. Our supporters kept coming up and saying, 'You've got to win today,' 'You must win,' 'Don't come off the field if you lose.' The Welsh were under exactly the same sort of pressure.

After such a build-up we didn't disappoint the supporters who had come to the bullring. The battle began in the first scrum as both packs smacked into each other. From that point it was just a matter of time before someone was sent off or carried off, or both, which in fact was the case. Even before Paul Ringer was sent off by David Burnett in the fifteenth minute, there were several outbursts and the referee had already issued a general warning. Paul Ringer's late tackle was indicative of the climate and mood of the game, but he had chanced his arm – this time into John Horton's face – once too often. That we applauded the referee and slow hand-clapped Paul Ringer off the field says all you need to know about what we thought of his behaviour. Even before the John Horton late tackle, he had been up to his tricks. Dusty went to collect a high ball and was bowled over by David Richards and Steve Fenwick; the ball went loose and Paul Ringer came charging through to put his knee into the small of Dusty's back. The John Horton affray was not nearly so bad, but Paul Ringer took no notice of his pre-match trial or the referee's general warning and carried on as a law unto himself.

If you expected his dismissal to ease the tension, then you were wrong. From the sending-off position, Dusty put us ahead, but Wales countered immediately when the English scrum lost control near its line and Jeff Squire beat Steve

Smith to the touch-down.

Well, we had one sent off ... who was going to be carried off? It turned out to be me! Nearing half-time I went back to gather a rolling ball and, as I gathered, I remembered the golden rule of keeping my back to the opposition to protect the ball and me. Suddenly everything went black as I thought my head was on its way between the posts. I realized that I had received a vicious kick to the head and, as I groggily got to my feet, I could feel the rough edge of flesh where my nose had been split open. There was blood everywhere.

The referee looked a bit horrified and Tony came over to me and said, 'Christ!' Off I went with Don Gatherer to the touch-line where my regular escort, Doctor Leo, was waiting. Mike Davis came down to the medical room, and after he also had looked aghast, I decided to have a look in the mirror at this horror. It wasn't a pretty sight and now I know what being battle-scarred means. Leo stitched up the wound; the skin was stretched tight and the whole area felt very tender. Mike asked if I wanted to go back. Stupidly for a moment I thought about it before common sense prevailed and I said no. Mike Rafter came on at half-time to replace me.

Go back to play in that? You must be joking! Scared? Too right. That first 40 minutes had knocked the stuffing right out of me. Coming off the field to take a detached view for a few minutes made the whole affair look like a brawl. There was very little rugby in this crazy game; everybody was at each other's throats and growling instead of watching the ball. People were giving 'verbal', being niggly, pushing and generally taking the fun out of rugby. The ball seemed the last concern.

I was interested to see on television what had necessitated my withdrawal from this cauldron. Very revealing it was, too. No wonder I was shaken. As I had gathered the ball, Geoff Wheel, with a full swing of the boot, had belted my head in a clumsy attempt to hit the ball. If I had faced him, instead of turning my back, there is no knowing what damage he could have done. How much of a face can they sew back on? Whether it was a deliberate action or not, I didn't know, but it certainly was in keeping with what had gone on before.

Looking in the mirror, I was worried about the kids. What would they say when they saw their father coming in the next day looking like this? How could I explain that I played rugby because I enjoyed it? As it was, typically, they took no notice at all.

Kris and my folks were watching the game; all this could not have been very pleasant for them. I felt very disillusioned as I put on my tracksuit and went to sit in the stand. What was the point? Everybody in the stand was agog, almost watching with their mouths wide open in amazement; like me, they couldn't believe all this was happening. The trouble hadn't stopped with my injury. Steve Fenwick completely lost his head and went in with arms and elbows flying; in the end, he lost Wales the game. Their captain, Jeff Squire, was also to blame. I've got a lot of time for Jeff, but you've got to control your side on the field. Instead, there was pandimonium from start to finish.

Dusty's second penalty took us ahead again, but Wales looked to have sneaked it yet again when Alan Phillips charged down Steve Smith's kick, gathered and fed Elgan Rees, who sped under the posts. Wales, as they had done all afternoon, missed the kick, but they were in front again. Then, in the dying minute, another Welsh indiscretion allowed Dusty Hare the chance of immortality as he slotted over the winning kick for a 9 points to 8 victory.

Rugby, though, was the big loser. Doctor Leo compared the scene in his medical toom to the TV series 'M.A.S.H.' Candidates for the use of the needles and thread after me were Steve Smith, Bill Beaumont, Maurice Colclough, John Scott and Wales's Alan Phillips. Both teams seemed rather stunned that the match had become the bloodbath that everybody had predicted. There was only one thing worse than playing in a game like this ... and that was playing in a game like this and losing.

Depressed we may have been but the realization slowly filtered through that we were one game away from the Grand Slam.

I bumped into Geoff Wheel in the tearoom and he offered by way of apology and explanation, 'Sorry, Rog; fifty–fifty see.' I wasn't going to argue the toss. In many ways Geoff's a 'big daft' lad who was so wound up by the whole occasion that he couldn't control himself. By a quirk of fate, the two Welsh players on a table with me and Tony at the dinner were Paul Ringer and Geoff Wheel. But as the Welsh normally do in a crisis, they became even more introverted and close-knit.

It was probably too early to judge the impact of our encounter. And the press, having got what they wanted, made full use of our war zone for material. At the time, I felt like giving the game up; there seemed little point in going on if rugby had degenerated into this. The injury to me was only a part of it; just one incident indicative of the way players were behaving; I was simply unlucky to be in the wrong place at the wrong time.

But our encounter was a thing of the past: the match was a one-off and the game against Scotland would offer a chance to make amends. There was a month until that Murrayfield visit and I needed all that time to get myself fit again. The Welsh game was a warning about the dangers of rugby if players forget their duty to the game and to each other.

If Twickenham was the agony, then Murrayfield was the ecstasy as rugby, and English rugby, found itself again. Rugby had only to wait a few weeks before the memory of Twickenham was exorcized by our thrilling attack display at Murrayfield.

The Grand Slam celebrations that evening weren't all bad; my sore head and sore ribs next morning told me that. Sitting in an almost deserted breakfast room, I obviously wasn't the worse offender, even though my appearance was an hour later than usual. After ordering the usual breakfast mountain, the Gloucester 'no-necks' trio – Messrs Mills, Blakeway and Sergeant – entered with a still dinner-jacketed John Scott, complete with the match ball. Our mood turned to panic when the waiter told us we had been left behind and the England coach had left for the airport an hour earlier. Once again the RFU's after-match organisation was to be found lacking. With the game over, our role became subservient again as we reverted to the position of minors on a school's outing. None of us had received the calls we'd ordered, nor had anyone on the coach thought it rather odd that several of the players were missing.

A 'follow-that-coach' taxi ride ensued and we reached the airport just in time. Not too happy with our lot, Don Rutherford and Col. Dennis Morgan received some sharp words about our neglect. But we had reckoned without the time-honoured traditions of the Rugby Football Union's code. In no uncertain manner we were informed that players, however important they might be before a game, were now reduced to the ranks of extras. All the talk on the plane back home was of the forthcoming British Lions' tour of South Africa; the 30 players going were to be announced tomorrow. Billy was a dead cert for captain and many of the team hoped to make the party. Tony Neary and I were unavailable for the trip with the excuse of 'business commitments' rearing its ugly head.

Since his debut at the Arms Park in 1971, many players had come and gone; but Tony Neary, apart from that selectorial insanity in 1977 and 1978, stayed. And with no slight intended to Bill Beaumont, it was Tony Neary who should have been the Player of this Grand Slam Year. If people had looked up from scrums, lines-out, rucks and mauls as often as I did during the 1980 campaign, then there would have been no contest. Tony was constantly there tackling, ripping the ball off opponents, driving on; always, always on the move, hounding and harassing poor fly-halves. And, even through the trials and tribulations, Tony remained his own man – you had to respect him even more for that. Now we were near the end of the road, but maybe we could do it again sometime.

12

The Way Ahead

While the Grand Slam was the pinnacle of success for England, many of the players were looking beyond to that British Lions tour. Sadly, circumstances outside the game conspired to make my participation impossible.

A fortnight after the Welsh débâcle, I was the guest speaker at a Sportwriters' lunch; the two obvious topics on the menu for discussion were of course violence and South Africa. It was put to me that the notorious clash at Twickenham would be nothing compared with the violence the Lions were likely to encounter in their eighteen matches on tour. I replied, 'If that happens, it would be sad and serious for the future of rugby. If I'm there I'll just pack my bags and swim home.' I did not necessarily believe that that would be the case, but I couldn't stomach another game like the Welsh match – which I compared with a 'festering boil which burst'. I had no doubts that my view on more violence would be 'enough's enough'.

At the time I was hoping to make the tour. I did give the moral implications concerning apartheid a lot more thought than I had in 1974, but I still came back to my basic belief that contact is better than isolation. I appreciated that others might hold different views, but expected them to respect my opinion as I did theirs. I also worried about revisiting the haunts of my youth – in rugby terms; things would not be the same and the 1980 British Lions would have to go a long way to emulate the achievements of Willie John McBride's men. Also, the physical hardships of those three months away might be too much for me after all my problems. But, taking everything into consideration, I decided that I would like to do it all again.

Yet just over a week later, I was on the phone to John Lawrence telling him for a second time that I wouldn't be making the Lions tour. The reasons were that Forward Health had been taken over earlier in the year by Shang International, a Hemel-based company which specialized in complete hospital packaging. The move had given us much more stability, but the first six months under new management were bound to be crucial. To spend twelve weeks away in South Africa repeating an experience was just not on in the circumstances. After a long chat with Ken Burgess, our new managing director, the final decision not to tour was taken. This was a natural choice and I haven't had any cause to regret it. Tony Neary was also unavailable, and likewise Paul Ringer (suspended) and Fergus Slattery, which meant the Lions were rather short of back-row forwards, especially with regard to pace.

England's thrilling Grand Slam finale ensured that many of the side would be touring South Africa. With Tony and I out of consideration, John Scott was the only member of the pack ignored; on reflection, his omission was a mistake. John Carleton, Mike Slemen and Clive Woodward were all given the nod among the backs, although we were disappointed that there was no place for Dusty Hare. The tour was littered with misfortunes and injuries and both Paul Dodge and Steve Smith flew out as replacements. Steve arrived for the last four days of the tour and didn't play a match, but I'm sure he managed to cram in a whole tour's enjoyment in those few hours. Bill Beaumont, as captain, Maurice Colclough and Peter Wheeler were all test regulars. Fran Cotton (at one time suspected of having had a heart attack) and Phil Blakeway were both home before the end of the tour.

The injuries contributed in a large part to the defeat in the test series, although elementary mistakes also led to the Lions' downfall.

Despite missing those experiences, the summer was still a busy time for me. Work was only part of it and I didn't spend my time longing for the high veld. After a holiday with the family in Majorca, where I swam a lot and generally toned myself up, I took part in 'Superstars', which had long been an ambition of mine. Peterborough was the venue for our heat and I regard those couple of days as the best sport I've ever enjoyed. The only other rugby star was Andy Ripley ... he was starting his journey to success in the British and European competition before taking third place in the world finals. We were joined by Gary Owen and Mike Channon from soccer, Desmond Douglas from table tennis, Dave 'Boy' Green from boxing and Konrad Bartelski from downhill skiing.

Although I picked up points in swimming, basketball and the gym tests, I let myself down badly in the canoeing and cycling, where I would have expected my previous experience to have given me the edge. Andy Ripley was quickly guaranteed first place as he left us mere mortals behind. It was left to the last event, the steeplechase, to decide whether Mike Channon or I was to be runner-up. Unfortunately, at my pace I was never in the hunt and was even unable to take advantage of the situation when Mike fell over the last hurdle. So I missed out on the British finals by a single point.

A couple of weeks later I was back attempting many of the same events, this time as a member of a rugby team that was meeting the challenge of the soccer boys. Tom Kiernan was the man in charge of looking after quite a lively bunch, which also included Tom Grace, Fergus Slattery, Gordon Brown Mike Biggar, J.J. Williams, Steve Fenwick, Andy Ripley and Tony Neary. We showed our superiority over the round ball men in no uncertain manner. Their team, which was managed by Ron Saunders, included Glen Hoddle, Duncan McKenzie and Kevin Reeves.

Around this time Don Rutherford invited Andy Ripley, young scrum-half Nigel Melville and I to play for Prinz George's fifteen against Norway in Copenhagen. My 1980–81 season started early when I went on my first non-international tour to visit Canada with Northumberland at the start of the country's centenary year. The informal atmosphere made for a relaxing time and I was looking forward to another season at home.

While the immediate reaction to our Grand Slam success had been 'At last we've done it; now we can retire happy', now we felt that it was necessary to prove that it wasn't a one-off victory and so the fifteen to a man were looking for a repeat performance. But a heavy business schedule meant that my training sessions became irregular. My back started playing up again, and even when I found time to train, the treatment couch began to take its place. I was now caught in a vicious circle which I was unable to break. With Northumberland in their centenary year, I again made the long trek north for the county championship Saturdays as we clinched the Northern group again. By now I was receiving treatment from Norman Anderson in Newcastle as well as from Terry back in Hemel. By the time those Northern group matches were finishing, my problems were coming to a head.

Then, after turning out for Stanley's against Oxford University in November, my condition improved and I was looking forward to Northumberland's semi-final challenge against Surrey at Gosforth. But my movements became restricted and, after treatment with Norman Anderson, both Steve Gustard and I withdrew from the side, which beat Surrey 12 to 6 to reach the final for the second time in three years. We hoped we were going to put up a better show against Gloucestershire down in Kingsholm that we had against Middlesex.

England's preparations for the championship were to begin on 13 December with the opening of the divisional matches. The North picked me at number eight and my opponent in that first match was to be none other than John Scott for the South and South West. To prepare myself properly for that I needed at least one good game under my belt beforehand.

That 'trial' against Rosslyn Park at Roehampton was to be my finale as a senior player. After wondering for years how I would come to a decision about finally giving it all up, I was to suddenly find out midway through the second half. With my back aching I was moving around like an old man; even bending down to pick up the ball from the base of the scrum was an impossible task. By embarrassing contrast, Andy Ripley in direct opposition to me was looking suprememly fit and was having a stormer. In my condition I was unable to provide him with much competition. We talked in the showers afterwards and I said that perhaps I'd had enough; I could not face a repetition of this sort of display the following week against John Scott.

Later that evening, as the pain got worse, I couldn't even drive myself home and the Wasps winger Ian Bell had to oblige. A night's sleep did little to ease my pain and so on Sunday I decided to delay the inevitable no longer. There was no point trying to hide behind my reputation. By telling the England selectors now they would have over a month to find a replacement and could use the divisional event for this purpose.

I rang up Malcolm Philips, one of the selectors, who knew all about my past history. I told him that I had been struggling for weeks and had used the day before as a fitness test, which I had failed miserably. Rather than prolong the agony, it was better for all concerned if I called it a day rather than disappoint everyone later on. I put the phone down and said to Kris, 'That's it; it's all over'. Although I felt relief that I had decided my fate at last, there was still a nagging doubt that maybe I might have been premature. Struggling to get out of my bed on Monday morning eased any worries about that.

On a playing level, though, I set my sights on getting ready for the county championship final at the end of January. I was bitterly disappointed over Christmas to realize that I was not going to make it. In such a special season, after so many memories of a decade with the county, I had hoped to take part in this fitting climax.

In many ways it was a grand finale, although my part was restricted to sitting in the stand. Northumberland had battled hard early on, but it looked as if the boot of Peter Butler would guarantee another success for Gloucestershire. In the end, two late tries ensured the right result for us. After my normal low profile and dead reaction at the height of any triumph some of my contemporaries looked amazed as I burst into the changing room behaving like an overgrown schoolboy. I understood the reaction of others in the past.

With that final over, there was nothing left for me to aim at and the logical conclusion was that my playing days were over. Although I felt better, the memory of struggling around over Christmas remained fresh. With my involvement, too, in sports injury, I was well aware that any further trouble might lead to permanent damage.

Watching the 1981 international championship was a revealing experience. Four days after I withdrew from consideration, so did Tony Neary, who had been troubled by a rib cartilage injury and also had business commitments which were becoming an increasing burden. The Grand Slam team's intention had been to stay together and bid for another championship title, but slowly that team was disintegrating. Fran Cotton, too, called it a day after leaving the field with a pulled hamstring in the opening game against Wales. Fran had fought back hard after his South African disappointments, but he decided he had had enough after this latest setback.

Despite Dusty Hare's 19 points, England went down by a couple of points against Wales, as the Leicester full-back failed to emulate his last-minute match-winning kick of the previous season. Tony and I had been replaced in the flank by Mike Rafter and newcomer David Cooke, with Moseley's Nick Jeavons replacing Mike for the remainder of the season. These two young players, although raw, will only get better with experience.

England had rather a mixed season, beating Scotland and Ireland, before failing to beat France in a bid to share the championship. The promise of years to come was seen in the outstanding debuts of fly-half Huw Davies and full back Marcus Rose, who both scored tries in their first England games. The summer tour to Argentina introduced rising stars Tony Swift, David Trick and Nigel Melville among the backs. Against the Pumas, Bill Beaumont and John Scott were the only two members of the Grand Slam pack left and the scrum is currently undergoing a transition period as the names of the seventies are replaced. But the side did exceptionally well to become the first home country to win a series in Argentina, drawing the first test and winning the second.

With my active participation a thing of the past, 1981 has given me a chance to reflect on what rugby has given me over the years. So much of my character has been shaped by what has happened in my rugby life. In the early days, I was grateful for being looked after; coming to terms with physical aggression and commitment did not come easily to me and there were several times when I wondered if my temperament was ideally suited to such a bruising sport.

The 1974 Lions tour was my finishing school. I was no longer prepared to allow myself to drift, letting the tide carry me along, and I tried to control my destiny – back willing. Just when I had overcome the struggle of establishing myself and felt secure in the knowledge that I was one of England's top forwards, my back condition appeared. It cast a shadow over the next seven years and was never far from my thoughts.

As well as the flesh not always being willing, the spirit could also be pretty weak, too, and I've been fortunate in having people around me who, in addition to giving support, have been tough with me and kept me going when my natural instincts may have been to give up. My parents, Bryn Jones, and now Kris, have all helped to give my life direction. I've also been fortunate with the coaches and players it has been my honour to be involved with. While I've explained earlier the reasons why I don't think John Burgess was successful with England, I have tremendous respect for him and what he gave to players like Fran Cotton, Tony Neary and myself. The North's ascendancy during this period was not due to one individual, but all my peers would agree that John's contribution was enormous. It is significant that Lancashire have only recently been able to find a comparative successor in Des Seabrook.

The most crucial turning point in my life was the move to the north east, first to college and then to live in Newcastle. And I was so fortunate that my arrival coincided with the emergence of both Gosforth and Northumberland.

I would not have missed being part of Gosforth's rise to the top for the world. The club has given me so many friends and happy moments, only some of which I've been able to relate in this book. I always treasure the memory of the company of Dave Robinson and Peter Dixon in the back row. I've already dealt with Peter, but Dave's role was equally important. His great zest for life became obvious early on when I got to know

185

him on England's 1971 Far East tour. I've been driven by many people in a variety of cars all over the world, but 'Robbo' takes the prize for producing the highest level of adrenalin amongst his passengers. Dave always felt that he should have played for England; he had the ability to, but after the lessons of the 1967 All Blacks visit, the hunt was on for big flankers. Now he's coaching Gosforth and still travelling the seventy miles from Cockermouth – which says everything about his loyalty to the club and total commitment to the game.

Playing for Gosforth meant that we had about one tough game a month; generally, we were in control from start to finish. This sort of preparation is hardly adequate for international rugby, when you get very few chances. During the lean years of the seventies, it became obvious to me that England would have to introduce a more competitive system if they were to have that degree of sharpness needed to survive. So many chances to score were squandered because we were simply not geared to react quickly enough.

That could be cured with a system where the best clubs in the country play each other. Even Gosforth, who undertake more travelling than most, only played three London clubs, Coventry and Bedford in the midlands, none in the south west and the remainder in the north, plus a few in Scotland. In a national side, players need to know each others' strengths and weaknesses, so that when they are under pressure on the field, there is an instinctive collective awareness of danger so that the area can be covered. Regular hard matches is the only answer. That would encourage the use of a pool of players ... which should in theory give more players exposure to the big time. That way it is to be hoped more talent that is currently wasted through lack of opportunity to express itself would come to the surface.

John Burgess's recent report about the game's standard made a lot of sense to me. Some of my most enjoyable games have been with the regional divisional sides; they allow you to play against players of equivalent standard. When Gosforth were at their peak, the incursion of the county championship programme could be a bind at times; I can well understand the feelings of Leicester, who are England's leading club at the

186

moment, in not supporting the county championship. But again, like the Mallaby Report, RFU have rejected those proposals put forward by a committee set up to examine the game. The Burgess report reflected the mood of rugby people up and down the country and was geared to putting England's considerable talent back on top. But it denounces the county system, and this the authorities would not accept. It will be interesting to see how the top clubs support the new-styled county championship this season.

In some ways it was a relief to retire from the big time. The pressures and demands had mounted increasingly throughout my career. Since I had played for England, and especially as captain, I hadn't really been able to call my life my own. Not that I minded – the game had given me a lot – but by the beginning of 1981 I had had enough.

My last year, especially, brought the question of violence to the forefront of the game. There had always been a fine line between what is acceptable and what is not. Everybody in the game has a basic responsibility to distinguish between good and – dare I say it – evil.

The clubs have to ensure that the small number of psychopaths who are allowed to slip through the net are generally ostracized from the game at the first hint of trouble. Players have an individual and corporate responsibility towards the game and each other. The referee, too, has to play his part as the thirty-first player: he must recognize the needs of the players, They in turn must accept his decision, and this is of fundamental importance.

Rugby, after all, is about the club and the friends you have made there. Although I was first capped for England in 1973 and made my last appearance against Scotland in 1980 to clinch the Grand Slam, I could just as easily have been playing for Seghill second fifteen. The amount of fun obtained by each type of player is roughly equal, the difference being the surroundings and experiences that have taken place.

One thing is certain; players have all been brought together by a common bond called rugby football. I hope it prospers and continues to offer youngsters the benefits and advantages it has been my great luck to enjoy.

Career Record

Blackpool GS – 1966–68
England Schools (19 Group) – 1968
    Lost to Wales 0–3; beat Scotland 15–3; drew with France
    11–11
Clubs: Fylde (1968), Gosforth (1968–79) and Wasps
    (1979–80)

England internationals

10.2.73	Ireland 18, England 9 (Dublin)
24.2.73	England 14, France 6 (Twickenham)
17.3.73	England 20, Scotland 13 (Twickenham)
15.9.73	New Zealand 10, England 16 (Auckland)
17.11.73	England 20, Australia 3 (Twickenham)
16.2.74	England 21, Ireland 26 (Twickenham)
2.3.74	France 12, England 12 (Paris)
16.3.74	England 16, Wales 12 (Twickenham)
1.2.75	England 20, France 27 (Twickenham)
15.2.75	Wales 20, England 4 (Cardiff)
15.3.73	England 7, Scotland 6 (Twickenham)
24.5.75	Australia 16, England 9 (Sydney)
31.5.75	Australia 30, England 21 (Brisbane)
8.1.77	England 26, Scotland 6 (Twickenham)
5.2.77	Ireland 0, England 4 (Dublin)
19.2.77	England 3, France 4 (Twickenham)
5.3.77	Wales 14, England 9 (Cardiff)
25.11.78	England 6, New Zealand 16 (Twickenham)
3.2.79	England 7, Scotland 7 (Twickenham)
19.1.80	England 24, Ireland 9 (Twickenham)
2.2.80	France 13, England 17 (Paris)
16.2.80	England 9, Wales 8 (Twickenham)
15.3.80	Scotland 18, England 30 (Murrayfield)

Uttley played at lock except for seven games at No. 8
(*v*. Wales, 1975, for the complete 1977 season, *v*. New

188

Zealand, 1978, and Scotland, 1979) and five games on the flank (*v*. Australia second test, 1975, and for the complete 1980 season). He captained England in the 1977 season and against Scotland in 1979. He scored two tries for England – *v*. Australia second test, 1975, and Scotland, 1977 (debut game as captain).

Tours

1971 Far East with England
1972 Selected for England tour of South Africa but withdrew because of injury and replaced by Chris Ralston
1973 New Zealand with England
1974 South Africa with the British Lions. Was selected as lock forward, but played in all four tests as a flank forward. The Lions won twenty-one games out of twenty-two, drawing the other one
1975 Australia with England
1977 Selected for the British Lions' tour to New Zealand, but withdrew because of injury and his place was taken by Jeff Squire

England record in the Championship

	P	W	L	D	For	Agst	Pos
1972	4	0	4	0	36	88	5th
1973	4	2	2	0	52	62	*
1974	4	1	2	1	63	66	5th
1975	4	1	3	0	40	65	5th
1976	4	0	4	0	42	86	5th
1977	4	2	2	0	42	24	3rd
1978	4	2	2	0	42	33	3rd
1979	4	1	2	1	24	52	4th
1972–79	32	9	21	2	341	476	
1980	4	4	0	0	80	48	1st

*All countries finished with two wins each, the first time this has ever happened.

189